You are respectfully invited
to return this book to
Gordon C. Fowler

The Giants of Sail

1919 – 1939

In the same 'Beken of Cowes' series :
The Glory of Sail   1897–1914

The Giants of Sail

1919 – 1939

by
Beken of Cowes

PHOTOGRAPHS BY FRANK AND KEITH BEKEN

Text by Alain Gliksman
in collaboration with
John Chamier and Jean-Michel Barrault

DODD, MEAD & COMPANY · New York

First published as *Les Géants de la Voile,* 1968
© Sté J.-L. Roth et Cie 1968
All translated material © Sté J.-L. Roth et Cie 1969
New material © Cassell & Co Ltd 1969

First published in the United States of America 1969
Library of Congress Catalog Card Number: 71-80825

Quotations have been taken, with kind permission of the copyright owners,
from the following:
Uffa Fox: *Sailing, Seamanship and Yacht Construction.*
                                    Peter Davies, London, 1934.
                    Sailing Boats. Newnes, London, 1959.
B. Heckstall-Smith: *The Britannia and her Contemporaries.*
                                    Methuen, London, 1929.
L. Francis Herreshoff: *The Common Sense of Yacht Design,* Vol. II.
                                    Rudder, New York, 1948.

Text phototypeset in Great Britain by
BAS Printers Limited, Wallop, Hampshire,
and printed in Paris by l'Imprimerie P.P.I.

Illustrations printed at Montrouge, France, by l'Imprimerie Draeger.
Bound in France.

FOREWORD

The Giants of Sail belong to another epoch—another world. Such giants were called *Meteor, Westward, Britannia* or perhaps *Shamrock* or *Endeavour*. Most of them were over 130 feet overall. They were run by hardcase skippers and tough, well-trained crews. Their owners were King George V, Vanderbilt, Kaiser Wilhelm II, Virginie Hériot or Sir Thomas Lipton. They spent fortunes in fitting out these wonderful hulls, in sails which set to perfection, in taking part in regattas which were spectacles of their kind, in the search for a fight afloat and the heady wine of victory. The schooners and the great cutters—the J Class and the pygmy (by comparison) 12-Metres—their halcyon days are gone. If this book evokes a memory of an Arthurian Age it should also remind us of our gratitude to that handful of sportsmen who strive to perpetuate this tradition. Yachting has become Sailing—and none the worse for that. Historically however the Giants of Sail would by now have passed from memory if it were not for talents and the unmatchable photographs of Frank and Keith Beken.

This is the second book in the *Beken of Cowes* series. To a certain degree it is a museum—a record of past glory and a witness of homage to those who raced in sail in the grand manner. But there is no dust about this museum. It is full of spray and wind, the changing lights of the jade Solent and the tough turmoil of its racing crews. The Beken genius has captured all this in the camera's eye—and preserved it for all posterity. This was indeed an Age—and one in which it was possible for a man's passion for the sport to come to full flower with little let or hindrance.

The Giants of Sail have gone. For most the idea of a big yacht now reaches no further than a 12-Metre and the America's Cup. Compared with most of the yachts pictured in this book a 12-Metre is a small boat, but it is nevertheless true that the struggles for the America's Cup have

FOREWORD (*continued*)

had a predominant influence on yacht racing. At the same time the search for formulae which allow dissimilar yachts to race against each other under handicap has been a continuous process. If the America's Cup has played a big part in the development of the big racing yacht, then in these other directions the different rules and ratings, wise or foolish, have united naval architects, builders and owners alike in efforts to get the maximum out of each and every equation as soon as it has been promulgated.

Surely nobody now knows how to cut sails from Egyptian Cotton like those sailmakers did fifty years ago? And does our brightwork really shine as if it has been given coat after coat of copal varnish, rubbed down and painstakingly burnished? Where is the sparkle of polished bronze and brass? Perhaps we smile at the skippers in these photographs, sporting their fierce moustaches beneath the peaks of their white-topped caps. But these men would take the wheel and race gunwhale to gunwhale to the turning buoy at twelve or thirteen knots, carrying 10,000 square feet of sail above them. That needed a cool head and a steady nerve. And, incidentally, the King of England was quite capable of taking his trick at the wheel in such company — and finishing first.

These prodigious giants would shock if it were not for their beauty. If, when turning over these Beken pages, you can imagine yourself aboard one of the great cutters storming majestically up the green Solent, remember too that they are here because of men's love for the Giants of Sail. Owners, captains and crews poured out money and effort on their yachts — but perhaps none lavished more care on them than the Bekens, who know how to seize the moment of truth, the most dramatic angle for a shot, and the photograph which shows a yacht in all her glory.

A.G.

The Giants

Beken of Cowes 1 closed with a photograph of two 12-Metre cutters, *Ierne* and *Alachie,* racing off Le Havre in the summer of 1914. For nearly five years there was no opportunity for the great ships to race against each other. Some indeed never raced again, and many of the fine seamen who crewed them did not live to see the peace that followed the holocaust of the First World War.

Until they entered the war in 1917, the Americans managed to keep many of the great yachts in commission, but when Frank Beken took up his camera again in 1919 and set out upon his beloved Solent waters, the social changes the war had enforced were already mirrored in them and reflected on both sides of the Atlantic. It is certainly easier for us to see the direct line of descent from those early post-First World War days to the yachting we know today, than it could have been to forecast then what was to happen. At that time there seemed still to be a spaciousness, a *style,* and few could have thought that it was doomed while the great yachts you will see in these pages flourished.

The great days of the schooners were already gone twenty years before the First World War; nevertheless, between the wars some devoted owners continued to keep a few schooners fitted out and in commission—witnesses and symbols of a more ample way of life—and matched them against the newcomers as you will see in these pages. The English cutters and the American sloops which took their place were just as big, even if perhaps they were of lesser displacement, and certainly they were faster. But it was all too good—and too expensive—to last, and in turn these giants had to give way to a new thoroughbred which appeared in modern dress on the eve of the Second World War. That was the 12-Metre—and our story has turned full circle.

Virginie Hériot and Ailée

THIS is the second of the *Ailées*. She belonged to the world's—*and* France's—most renowned yachtswoman, Virginie Hériot. To this day the Dragons race for the Coupe Virginie Hériot. This *Ailée* was designed by Charles E. Nicholson and built at his Gosport yard in 1928. The most interesting thing about the photograph—apart from its picturing a truly magnificent yacht—is the rig; that of a three-masted staysail schooner. It is not an efficient sail plan—there are so many 'gaps' in it—and usually it needs a gale of wind to give the hull beneath it any real drive. It saved manpower however since the sails comprising the rig could be designed as smaller units capable of being handled by a smaller crew. In 1928 in the wake of the First World War with its harvest of death and social change crews were already at premium. So this was the rig that Charles Nicholson put into *Ailée II*. You can see exactly the same rig today in Stavros Niarchos's *Creole*.

Year of build:	*1928*
LOA:	*167 ft. 8 in.*
LWL:	*122 ft.*
Beam:	*28 ft. 6 in.*
Draft:	*15 ft. 6 in.*
Sail area:	*Unknown*
Tons TM:	*495*

Cetonia

CETONIA was a big boat. Lloyd's Register lists her as having been designed by G. M. Soper and built under the name *Esperance* by Camper & Nicholson at Gosport in 1902. Her Thames Tonnage was 295 and her length between perpendiculars (stem to rudderhead, for Thames Measurement purposes) was 120 feet. Her beam was 24 feet, she drew 15 feet 9 inches and set 7,990 square feet of sail. The first four years of her existence are veiled in mystery and one has the impression that for one reason or another completion of her construction was delayed. However in 1906 she came into the ownership of Lord Iveagh who renamed her *Cetonia* and kept her for fifteen years. Her next owner was Gilbert A. Tonge and then in 1929 Lord Stallbridge acquired her in an executor's sale, parting with her just before the Second World War. It is interesting to note that the price Lord Stallbridge was asking for her in 1934 when he was thinking of selling was only £4,000 ($16,000). Her original sail plan was that of the classical two-masted schooner but she later appeared as we see her here, a three-masted staysail schooner. In this Beken photograph she is reaching eastwards past Old Castle Point at Cowes. The bone in *Cetonia*'s teeth indicates a stiffening breeze, but she is carrying all plain sail under the low cloud base and threatening sky. Note the square racing flag worn at the *mizzen* truck. As the height of her spars shows, *Cetonia* wasn't really a racing boat. Nevertheless she was a particularly successful cruiser.

Year of build:	*1902*
LOA:	*120 ft. (T.M.)*
LWL:	*123 ft.*
Beam:	*24 ft.*
Draft	*15 ft. 9 in.*
Sail area:	*7,990 sq. ft.*
Tons TM:	*295*

Bluenose

◀ Year of build: 1920
LOA: 143 ft.
LWL: 112 ft.
Beam: 27 ft.
Draft: 15 ft.
Sail area: 9,987 sq. ft.
Tons TM: 285

THE GRAND Banks schooner—few types of vessel have so appealed to the imagination. No matter the hard prosaic life of their crews, the pursuit of King Cod off Newfoundland has produced its own heroic image to fire the dreams of lesser men. The sailing men of New England and Nova Scotia to the south and north of the American–Canadian border have often been called the best in the world. One can't see this being much of an exaggeration. Line fishing from cockleshell dories in icy squalls and always at risk of losing contact with their 'mother ships' in sudden fog, the Grand Banksmen, their faces blue with cold, may indeed lay claim to the highest of all reputations as seamen. And as soon as the schooners' holds were full they would make for port, racing each other every inch of the way for the heady satisfaction of beating the other crews as much as for the commercial rewards of being first with fish on the quays.

Shoal waters are always 'unhealthy'. But in these waters is added the juxtaposition of the Gulf Stream and the Labrador Current which complicates navigation and brings fog one day in three. Icebergs are an ever-present menace. The low-lying, sandy coast is a permanent trap for ships. Only real sailors could possibly make old bones out there. In the lists of schooners sailing out of Lunenburg and Halifax and Gloucester the final date on the record is just as often that of a shipwreck as of a voyage to the breaker's yard. The Grand Banksmen had very definite ideas about sailing as a sport. There was nothing but contempt amongst them when it was learned that in the 1920 America's Cup matches both defender and challenger had asked for the postponement of one race because that morning the wind had reached 30 knots.

In 1920 the Canadian W. H. Davis had fallen in with the general wish by putting up an international cup reserved for the great fishing schooners, the Fisherman's Trophy. From either side of the American–Canadian frontier there were eliminating races to find opposing champions. That same year off Halifax the American schooner *Esperanto* out of Gloucester beat the Canadian and went home with the cup and a substantial money prize. This defeat was felt an intolerable humiliation by the men of Lunenburg, who had put up the losing Canadian champion. Straight away they set themselves to the job of getting their revenge, and in the following year *Bluenose* slid down the ways and a legend was launched.

(PAGES 12–13 AND 19–22)

Westward

Year of build: 1910
LOA: 135 ft.
LWL: 96 ft.
Beam: 27 ft.
Draft: 16 ft. 5 in.
Sail area: 13,483 sq. ft.
Tons TM: 323

▶

L OOKING ahead somewhat in our account of the career of *Bluenose*, there was during her 1935 visit to British waters a famous race round the Isle of Wight, in which she was beaten by the giant veteran *Westward*, owned then by T. B. F. Davis. He was widely known as 'Butcher Davis', a man whose visiting cards bore the inscription 'T. B. F. Davis—East and South Africa', and nothing more. He had the reputation—and it was not exaggerated—of having the most effective vocabulary of the whole yachting scene. If Virginie Hériot represented the Latin passion for the sea, here in T. B. F. Davis was the Anglo-Saxon equivalent, less subtle, more direct, more physical—but just as much a living thing.

Davis bought *Westward* at the beginning of 1920 and became greatly attached to his vessel. He lived on board, maintained her with every care and pulled his weight with the best in the refits which he had carried out by his crew. *Westward* was in his ownership for twenty-six years, right up to his death in 1946—but he was pre-occupied with her future a long time before that. So it happened that under the terms of Davis's will, *Westward* was towed from Dartmouth on 14 July 1947 by the tug *Portwey* and sunk in 93 fathoms in the Hurd Deep. Doubtless there was pride and egoism in contriving this gesture, but anyone who has seen a fine ship put to death in a breaker's yard will understand it.

Westward was one of the largest yachts ever to race. When all the other schooners had gone the photographs show her fighting it out with the cutters and in no way being left behind. The photograph shows that her rig and sails were in perfect racing trim. As for the way she was driven one may have full confidence in her owner—and the more so since the story goes that *Westward* would only call at ports with a naval base because this way she was able to bring her crew up to full racing strength by hiring seamen from the Navy who were off duty or on leave. And looking at the size of the sails and the height of the spars one can believe the story.

(PAGES 16–17 AND 29)

The Deck of Bluenose

On the well-scrubbed deck the nests of fishing dories are stowed and idle. They were probably very much in the way during *Bluenose*'s prestige visit to Britain for the Silver Jubilee of King George V and Queen Mary in 1935. But those same dories were eloquent witness to the pride and competence in their work of the Canadian fishermen of the Grand Banks. The lowering sky and the implicit violence of the elements contrast strongly with that white cap cover in the centre of the picture and the relaxed attitudes of the crew in the foreground. Here the whole grandeur of the great age of sail is evoked — a dangerous and often brutal existence, lived out by calm and competent men.

Bluenose

BLUENOSE was a pure product of Nova Scotia. Her designer was W. J. Roue of Halifax, who was self-taught and whose 'Bible' was *Yacht Architecture* by Dixon Kemp. Roue's sole interest was in yachts and the craft of the sailing fishing fleets. Smith & Rhuland's yard at Lunenburg built her as they had built so many other Grand Bankers, of Nova Scotian timbers — pine, oak, spruce, birch. Only their masts came from more distant parts — they were Oregon pine.

There was no doubt in anyone's mind that *Bluenose* was destined for fame. On the day her keel was laid the Duke of Devonshire, the Governor-General of Canada, came to drive home a ceremonial golden nail. However the Duke was a little early and a few drinks were taken to keep him in patience. Unfortunately by the time it came to drive the spike the Governor's eye was out and his first blow missed. The others were no better directed and in the end some less august guest charged himself with the job of hammering the famous nail home. . . .

Launched on 26 April 1921, *Bluenose* sailed straight into a remarkable career. Trampling over all other contenders for the honour she qualified to challenge for the International Fisherman's Trophy and walked off with it by the length of a street. During the next fifteen years she was the undisputed champion of the Grand Banks schooners. For year after year she held the trophy, which counted above all others with Canadian sailors, beating back five American challengers of which no less than three were specially commissioned from the drawing-boards of top designers for the express purpose of regaining the trophy.

These feats did nothing to interfere with the schooner's job of earning her daily bread season after season, fishing on the Grand Banks, and in the course of this day-to-day business she broke the record for a catch into the port of Lunenburg.

Nor did the occupational hazards of her trade pass *Bluenose* by, though one could easily believe that they occurred merely to highlight her exceptional career. On her maiden voyage she was nearly laid aboard by a three-masted square-rigger. Then, overtaken by a sudden gale when at anchor with Sable Island under her lee, she was able to escape the trap and claw her way off to windward. In 1930 she went ashore in Placentia Bay, Newfoundland. For four days she was pinned to the rocks while waves carried away her rig and the boats which served her. As her followers had come to expect, she got away.

Bluenose became a national symbol, appearing on postage stamps and on medallions. In 1933 she appeared on Lake Michigan and at Chicago where she represented Canada at the Century of Progress Exposition, and in 1935 there was another 'ambassadorial' at an even more distinguished level. In that year she crossed the Atlantic officially to represent Canada at the Silver Jubilee celebrations of King George V and Queen Mary. The famous schooner was welcomed triumphantly at Plymouth and Cowes, where English yachtsmen hurried aboard her where she lay at anchor, with her full fishing gear and the dories stacked on her deck. She also featured in the Fleet Review which was one of the last official duties which the King was destined to carry out and, fishing gear and all, challenged the cream of the home country's yachting fleet.

Bluenose and her crew took all these official ceremonies phlegmatically, if not with a real pinch of salt, but it was her Captain who always put the finishing touches to the story of *Bluenose* and indeed always made her seem rather larger than life. Angus Walters was small, wrinkled, excitable and was known as a 'butcher of sailcloth' in a land where that title took a bit of getting. He went to sea at thirteen as a cabin boy on his father's schooner in trade and fishing to the islands girdling the Caribbean Sea.

Bluenose (continued)

At the Jubilee Review, Angus Walters was invited aboard the Royal Yacht and was received by the King and his three sons, the Prince of Wales and the Dukes of York and Kent. His comment?

'He was a great man and we had a bit of a chat. He'd heard about *Bluenose* and showed a lot of interest in herrings. But the Prince of Wales leaned across to the King and said that I fished for cod rather than herring, so the King told me to stand by his side for the photograph. Then we had a little more chat—and then I came back on board.' The yachtsman King let it be known that he would have liked to board *Bluenose*, but he had had to leave Cowes earlier than anticipated and sent his regrets to the Captain. 'I was desolated,' commented Walters. 'I wanted to offer him a dram and since we had no alcohol aboard, I'd sent ashore specially to buy a bottle of King George Whisky.'

Of the huge and redoutable *Westward* and the race round the Isle of Wight, the quote is, 'Sure they beat us, but hell! we gave them a good run for their money.'

Bluenose returned to Canada, but typically not before fighting out a four-day gale which sent her back into Falmouth with her boats gone, her steering broken and sundry other damage. In 1938 after yet more successes she was feted by the Lunenburgers, the schools were closed, there was a procession of decorated cars and floats, and bands played Captain Angus Walters and his crew up and down the streets of the town.

Nothing less than a World War was able to blur the Nova Scotians' memories of *Bluenose*. But by then time had in any case run out for the sailing schooner in the fishing industry. *Bluenose* weighed heavily in her owners' budgets. One day posters appeared telling the world that she was for sale. Captain Walters, her one and only Captain throughout her active life, rallied all his resources, trying without success to establish a subscription list to keep his precious schooner in her native land. In 1942, shorn of her proud spars, she was sent to trade between the Caribbean Islands. One Sunday in January 1946, a brief radio flash was to stun any number of Canadians and to revive memories which they had thought long buried at sea. 'The schooner *Bluenose*', gave out the laconic voice of the announcer, 'has been lost on the coast of Haiti.' Few of her former adversaries had made it as far as the breaker's yard. *Mayflower* was wrecked, *Esperanto* was lost on the Sable Island just as was *Columbia*, who took twenty-two men with her when she went down. The *Henry Ford* went to the bottom off Newfoundland's Point Martin and *Elsie* off Saint-Pierre. The most dangerous rival, the *Gertrude L. Thebaud*, was lost close by the shore where *Bluenose* made her own grave.

Among the people of Lunenburg, innured to tales of shipwreck as they were, there soon grew a feeling that this particular one ought and should have been avoided. Tourists in ever-increasing numbers were coming to their town demanding to visit the place where the celebrated schooner was preserved. It was too late then to heed her Captain's plea.

That is the *Bluenose* story—a boat immensely loved and deserving that love, forgotten for an instant and lost almost at the same moment of time, and the loss bitterly regretted thereafter.

But it is, after all, a story that has a kind of happy ending. The Lunenburgers decided to resuscitate their proud vessel. In the same shipyard, many of the same workmen, labouring under the same designer, would build the same vessel, and on 24 July 1963, before a great crowd and in the presence of a representative of the Government, old Captain Walters, miraculously spared, presided over the launching of *Bluenose II*.

(PAGES 12–13 AND 19–22)

*Westward will forever remain the most famous of
the racing schooners. She was designed for
Mr. A. S. Cochran by one of the all-time greats of
naval architecture, Nathaniel Herreshoff, and built
at his yard at Bristol, Rhode Island, in 1910. As
his racing skipper, Mr Cochran had the redoubtable
Charlie Bevis. Before the 1914 war, she attracted
the eye and the maritime aspirations of the Kaiser
Wilhelm II and came into the ownership of the
Verein Seefahrt Hamburg, an organisation which
often appears in these pages, under the name
Hamburg II. The first Hamburg was the
America's Cup defender Rainbow.*

The Giants

ARE THERE words to add to the picture on pages 30–31? What a
wealth of patience went to catch *Britannia, Astra, Shamrock V*
and *Candida* in this majestic line abreast. The owners of these
incredible machines may have had devious and obscure motives
for ownership — that's certain. That pride was one of these — that's quite
possible. But indisputably there was a passion, a devouring passion not
confined to the privileged who were able to pay for such magnificent
vessels but which touched everyone remotely connected with them!
The designers, the builders, the riggers, the blacksmiths and sailmakers
working always to the limit of their materials and intuitively drawing
the maximum grace and beauty from them; the crews built up by years of
practical seamanship and their skippers, whose like will never be seen
again; and of course the Bekens.

'Probably some manifestation of a collective nature cult worshipping
the Godheads of Sun, Wind and Water' will be the guess of the archæolo-
gists several centuries hence when they drag this document from the
ruins left by the last politician. Will they be so very wrong?

(PAGES 30–31)

Gaff v. Bermudian Rig

SHAMROCK III leads *White Heather*, *Cambria* and *Candida*. This photograph cannot fail to raise a smile. It was taken in 1929. In a brisk sou'easter right on the nose, the two gaff-rigged cutters lead the two Bermudian-rigged ones which have been forced to reduce sail. Certainly their hulls would have been capable of standing up to more canvas, but in those days they had to nurse the 'marconi' mast. This was *Candida*'s first season and *Cambria*'s second.

White Heather was the second boat of this name designed by Fife for the famous yachtsman Myles B. Kennedy. She illustrates the 23-Metre Rule which she raced successfully.

(PAGES 32–33)

◀ **SHAMROCK III**
Year of build:	1903
LOA:	134 ft. 4 in.
LWL:	89 ft. 10 in.
Beam:	23 ft.
Draft	19 ft.
Sail area:	14,154 sq. ft.
Tons TM:	278

◀ **WHITE HEATHER**
Year of build:	1929
LOA:	95 ft.
LWL:	77 ft.
Beam:	20 ft. 4 in.
Draft:	11 ft.
Sail area:	Various
Tons TM:	179

◀ **CAMBRIA**
Year of build:	1928
LOA:	100 ft.
LWL:	75 ft.
Beam:	20 ft. 6 in.
Draft:	——
Sail area:	——
Tons TM:	162

◀ **CANDIDA**
Year of build:	1929
LOA:	117 ft.
LWL:	79 ft.
Beam:	20 ft. 5 in.
Draft:	14 ft. 4 in
Sail area:	——
Tons TM:	174

The Birth
of a Yacht

The Building of Endeavour

THE J Class boat building here is *Endeavour*, ever to be remembered as the yacht which came closest to winning the America's Cup. A boat which was a faster one than the New York Yacht Club defence could muster, and perhaps the only challenger ever to have a definite design edge over a Cup defender. The Americans saved the 1934 series by the skin of their teeth, superior tactical ability—and sheer good luck.

In the photograph on the left the plates of the steel topsides are going up. The deck beams and the floor bearers are in position—the photograph is taken from forward looking aft—and in the foreground to the right of the picture is the portable forge which kept the rivets hot. It was operated by apprentice shipwrights.

In our days riveting has been succeeded by welding, but when we admire the hull of one of these steel giants we may well spare a thought for the art and skill with which rivets were punched home—*and faired off*. The picture on the right shows the start of the laying of the pine deck over the steel deck beams.

(SEE ALSO PAGES 44–45)

The Racing Season—1929

SHAMROCK V ▶
Year of build: 1930
LOA: 120 ft.
LWL: 81 ft.
Beam: 19 ft. 7 in.
Draft: 14 ft. 8 in.
Sail area: 7,530 sq. ft.
Tons TM: 163

Roughly speaking, a racing yacht is put into commission early in May. She remains in commission until the first week in September. If a yacht owner decides to put in a whole season, he will begin racing about the end of May and finish at the end of August. During that time he will sail about forty races. The usual routine is to begin on the Thames estuary and at Harwich, and then go to Dover. Next the yachts proceed round Land's End to the Welsh coast and Kingstown. Then to the Firth of Clyde, where early in July they race for a fortnight. Thence to Belfast Lough and back down the St. George's Channel, round the Longships to Falmouth. Up the English Channel to the Solent for Cowes Week and the height of the holiday season beginning early in August. . . . At Cowes much of the best yacht-racing takes place, and we race every day. . . .

After the close of the Solent season the racing fleet proceeds to Bournemouth, Weymouth Bay, Plymouth Sound, Torbay, and Dartmouth.

If a yacht owner goes the round of all these regattas with his racing yacht, it will be gathered that he not only sails some forty races, but his yacht has made about 1,500 miles of sea passages besides in the course of the three-and-a-half or four summer months.

Added to this, during the times of which I have written . . . the *Britannia* sailed in the spring of the year from Cowes to the Riviera and back and raced in the south of France. *Britannia* and *Ailsa* thus sailed sixty races in one year.

This was a heavy strain on the scantlings of the yachts and their gear and upon the crew.

The average yacht-race for large yachts is about 40 miles, and takes about five hours. The crew have to begin to get ready for racing at six o'clock in the morning, and they have not finished their job and stowed away until tea-time or later.

Whatever size a racing yacht may be—if she is large enough to go this round of regattas I have named—the owner of the yacht should be able to live on board her with comfort. The smallest racing yacht at the present time which can be used as a residential home is a 'Twelve-Metre', about 21 or 23 tons displacement and 35 tons Thames tonnage. The largest class at the present time is the '24-Metre Class'.

A 24-metre is about 120 tons displacement and 175 tons Thames tonnage. The 12-metre is 41 to 43 feet long on the waterline, and the 24-metre about 76 to 80 feet. The *Britannia* is 159 tons displacement, 221 tons Thames measurement, and 88 feet on the waterline. The rules of the Y.R.A. provide that all large racing yachts must be classed at A1 Lloyd's and properly fitted internally with cabins. The larger racing yachts are most comfortably fitted and have every luxury. Bath rooms, electric light, and a deck house, living and sleeping cabins of perfect comfort, equal to those of modern cruisers and greatly superior to those of old-fashioned cruising yachts. In some of the smaller racing yachts, I am sorry to say, the *spirit* of the Y.R.A. rules with regard to cabins is not fairly carried out. In the competition to save weight internally, and thus get more lead ballast on the keel, the designers are apt to skimp the cabin fittings, and barely comply with the *letter* of the Y.R.A. rules instead of their spirit and intention.

The owners of such boats do not personally use their racing yachts as homes, but are wealthy men who live on board steam or motor yachts, and merely use their 12-Metre yacht for racing.

This evasion of the rules has always been a very bad thing for the sport of yacht-racing, because it is all against the class of yachtsmen who take the greatest personal interest in their boats, i.e. the owners who live aboard their boats and use them as homes. It favours the richer man who can afford to maintain both a racing yacht and a steam or motor yacht also, and it militates against the chances of the poorer man who wishes to use his racer as a residence.

B. Heckstall-Smith: *The Britannia and her Contemporaries*. 1929

Shamrock V

OPENED out, this photograph gives an unusual view of *Shamrock V*, the first boat actually built to the rules of the J Class. She was composite built, that is timber planking on steel frames, to the designs of the legendary Charles E. Nicholson. Although decisively beaten by *Enterprise* in her America's Cup challenge, she was a fine yacht and played a prominent part in the J Class scene. After Lipton's death in 1931 she passed into the ownership of T. O. M. Sopwith who, when he went into building the *Endeavours*, sold her to another British aircraft manufacturer, Richard Fairey. Another photograph of her at her launching can be seen on pages 48–9.

The Launching of Endeavour   ▶

FARTHER on in this book, on pages 48–9, there is a photograph of the launching of *Shamrock V* at the Camper & Nicholson yard at Gosport in 1930. *Shamrock* was the last of the Lipton dynasty. Here with *Endeavour* is the start of a new epoch (1934) although it was to be much shorter lived than its predecessor. Designed and built by Charles E. Nicholson for T. O. M. (Tommy) Sopwith, a great aeroplane builder and a dedicated helmsman, only a long run of ill luck blocked his way to regaining the America's Cup. First there was a strike by his crew for an increase in pay. Sopwith refused. Only nine stayed with *Endeavour* and the gaps were filled by amateurs in a dramatic 'pierhead jump'. They did their best but their sail handling could possibly never have been as perfect as that of the Americans aboard the defending *Rainbow*. Certainly their hands found the handling of wire sheets hard. For all that *Endeavour* won her first two races—and won them well. In the third race Sopwith, out in front and within sight of the finish, made two additional legs in order to cover *Rainbow*. But the wind was very light and these manœuvres killed *Endeavour*'s way and *Rainbow* ghosted past her to leeward. In the fourth race Sopwith, once again out in front, luffed to cover *Rainbow*. At *Rainbow*'s wheel was Vanderbilt and he held his course without wavering an inch. Rather than cut the American in two Sopwith broke off the luff and bore away. His subsequent protest was rejected for reasons that seemed specious to many. In the last race, the fifth, the challenger was caught the wrong side of a wind shift and given, as the French politely say, 'le coup de pied de l'âne'.

Like challengers before her, *Endeavour* retraced her wake across the Atlantic to serve as the hare for the next course.

Rainbow was at one and the same time one of the last works of Starling Burgess and the first rung of the ladder which was to hoist Olin Stephens on his way to being the greatest yacht designer of a new era.

The Launching of Endeavour (continued)

Year of build:	1934
LOA:	129 ft. 11 in.
LWL:	83 ft. 3 in.
Beam:	22 ft.
Draft:	15 ft.
Sail area:	—
Tons TM:	205

BEFORE the eyes of hundreds of spectators this superb yacht takes to her natural element. A launching is always an event but the hopes which went with this yacht, built for Tommy Sopwith's America's Cup challenge, heightened the intensity of this particular moment.

This is one of those rare occasions when we are able to study the underwater lines of the challenger, normally a closely guarded secret. All around *Endeavour* the photographers are clicking away and over on the left of her a 'lady-photographer' is to be seen. We wonder if her photograph survives. One cannot help being struck by the contrast between the pure and efficient hull lines of *Endeavour* and the angular aspect of the sheds in which she took shape: Right up to the last moment a J Class yacht 'belonged' to the people who built her, and these huge boats can rightly be described as being hand made.

In our day and age the most formidable racing machines are perhaps to be found among the shaky multihulls. *Sic transit. . . .*

Shamrock V

T HE LAUNCHING of *Shamrock V*, seen on the following two pages, must have been an exceptional occasion. At the age of 81, Sir Thomas Lipton was playing his last card in his fight for the America's Cup as *Shamrock V* slides down the slipway at Camper & Nicholson's yard at Gosport in June 1930.

Her deck is peopled with her crew and with yard workmen. The shore and the quay are crowded with spectators, every one of whom wished the new effort well with all their hearts. Even the roof of Ratsey & Lapthorn's sail loft has its precariously perched onlookers adding their cheers.

A launching such as this involved the whole town. Everything that could float was brought to the scene. In this picture, beneath *Shamrock's* shapely counter and against the quay wall, can be seen one of the early outboard motors. Sir Thomas Lipton's challenge was issued under the burgee of the Royal Ulster Yacht Club and the Blue Ensign defaced with the red Hand of Ulster flies in the early summer breeze.

Two months later another such yacht, *Enterprise*, left her slipway on the far side of the Atlantic. Lipton's splendid effort, seen here, was only to bring one further humiliation. Sportsmanship and sheer enthusiasm were not enough to create victory. In the end the Americans built four yachts and their hard fought trials for the honour of defending the Cup forged a final defence of such elaboration and high tune that the Cup races themselves turned out to be mere formalities.

(PAGES 48–9 AND 39–42)

The Beauty of Racing—1929

Much of the beauty of the sport of yacht-racing lies in its variety and uncertainty. If we race at twenty different ports on the coast, each course is utterly different, and calls for a variety of qualities in the vessel. Many points are tested, the vessel herself is tested by long reaches in smooth water, short tacking along the edge of a sandbank against wind and tide, or through a narrow channel between two sands when she must be very quick in stays to make the short boards. There is the long run under spinnaker, the long close-hauled punch, the broad reach with a tremendous breeze trying the maximum speed. The short head sea which shakes the ship at every punch, the long, easy, but big sea met with off Dover in which a short-keeled yacht may lose speed through the difficulty of steering. Then again the light, calm days, with scarcely a breath of wind on the water and light variable airs aloft, wherein one yacht may suddenly gain a huge and unexpected lead. Such a day is still further complicated by a rolling swell which shakes the wind out of the sails, or a tide which compels us to drop the kedge. The racing season tests helmsmanship in many phases. The art of manœuvring for position at the start between the five-minute guns requires nerve and judgment. The helmsman must jockey for position, and be fair to his opponents, and not over jealous to get the best position. There comes later on the planning or working out of the tacks 'keeping between your next opponent and the mark' if you are ahead, or 'keeping your wind clear' when you may be astern, a series of manœuvres which are as many in their permutations as those of a game of chess. Pilotage must play an important part at many of these ports, but none at all at others. Whilst every day there is the same importance in trimming the sails and handling them smartly. Rounding the marks in the course, and setting the course for the next mark is not merely a matter of navigation or reckoning in a yacht-race, the amount lost or gained is often dependent upon the manœuvres of one's opponent or opponents. The prize is of comparatively small monetary value, and there is no betting upon yacht-racing. . . .

A landsman asked me, 'What is there to describe in a yacht-race? When you have described one,' said he, 'you have told the story of them all.' To such ignorance of the sport of yacht-racing the sailor is hardly able to reply except in nautical and unparliamentary language. It is impossible for any two yacht-races to be alike. Few possess similar conditions.

The day's sport is long. When it is over, and evening in the still anchorage has come, our opponents arrive alongside and join us in the saloon, cigars are lit, George the steward places the whisky and soda on the table, and we fight the battle over again under the cabin lamp. The racing cutters are the chief object of interest at all the yachting ports they visit, local yachtsmen have the opportunity of seeing them only once a year, and the discussion of their quality and appearance runs high as soon as the tall masts come into harbour and anchor chains rattle through the fair leads. Yachtsmen love a yarn, the cruising men criticize the tall masts and slender rigging of the racers, and tell us that we ought to have high bulwarks, which in racing we do not want because they would scoop up the water and wet us deep every time we tack. The cruising yachtsman is apt to forget that to make our racing port we too have been cruisers, and have cruised a thousand miles.

B. Heckstall-Smith: *The Britannia and her Contemporaries*. 1929.

Portrait of a J Class Skipper

Amateur and Professional Skippers

OFTEN I am asked how I think a top notch amateur compares with a good professional. They are birds of such a different colour that there is no means of comparison. While a good amateur like Mr. Adams can often nurse a small yacht up to windward better than the professional, still all amateurs that I have seen are a joke in training the crew on a large yacht. Charlie Barr, after he had been captain of three cup defenders, could pick a crew every one of whom was particularly adapted to his duties and every one of the crew had perfect confidence in his captain. One of the peculiarities of Captain Barr was that he had a most remarkable memory. He could remember the exact details of an hundred races or so and most of the mistakes he or his competitors had made, and this in itself made him a scientific tactician. When he was at the wheel of a large yacht in a race he didn't need chart, racing circular, tide tables, or other paraphernalia, for their contents had been memorized and stowed away neatly in his head where he could automatically draw forth the needed information instantly in spite of wind, rain or darkness. If the regatta committee boat hoisted a signal he would know at once what it meant, and would know the compass bearing for most any course a yacht might take in the region he was racing. No doubt he could give out of his head the approximate soundings most anywhere near the race course. All I know is that life on board a yacht with Charlie Barr as captain was a perfect delight. You knew he was prepared for every occasion and the minor things in yachting etiquette were faultlessly attended to.

It has been said some years in the past when Mr. Adams did not show up at Marblehead that 'race week at Marblehead without Charles Francis Adams is like Shakespeare without Hamlet.' But if this can be said to be so, then racing yachts without a Charlie Barr could be likened to attempting the Passion Play without a Christus.

L. Francis Herreshoff: *The Common Sense of Yacht Design*. Vol. II, 1948.

CLOSE COMPANY

The Big Boats in close company—and at a buoy as well. Velsheda is out in front with Shamrock V on her starboard quarter. Charging in on port tack with the buoy close under her port bow is Astra. These yachts were moving at a smart pace and one hopes that Astra had room to tack when she cleared the buoy. No collision was reported so presumably she did—but she must have been well and truly sat on by the two starboard tack yachts.

(PAGES 52–3)

The majestic Britannia leads the class up-Solent from the west. Astern of her is Shamrock V—and there are in fact three others tailing away into the distance, with the last of them practically lost to sight in the haze. Britannia sets one of the 'ventilated' spinnakers which enjoyed a short period of favour and fashion. But spinnakers were soon to be set round the forestay and become 'parachutes' or 'ballooners'.
(PAGES 60–1)

Candida

Candida crosses the finishing line. The very instant is important because in handicap racing every split second counts. A crewman stands up forward with his arm raised to signal to his crouching, tensed-up comrades when the line is broken and the race over. Then, and only then, can they relax and make their way to the mooring.

A Race aboard Britannia—1921

SOME racing days . . . live in our memory. I will tell the story of one or two racing days in the old *Britannia*. . . . I will recall one race in particular, when the *Britannia* sailed in a very light wind much faster than any of the modern yachts. It was a red-letter day, and when I come to think of it, it was one of the few days when Sir Philip Hunloke did not take the wheel throughout the race, because we had another helmsman for a good many miles. His Majesty the King took the helm.

This is the little story of the race. It was on Saturday, 16 July, 1921, from Southend to Harwich. The competitors were:

Britannia	..	..	83·82 feet rating
White Heather	..	..	74·87 feet rating
Nyria, in her Bermudian-rig		72·87 feet rating

The additional sail and hoist planned by Mr. Alfred Mylne had raised the *Britannia*'s rating by the rating rule then in force from 82·03 feet in 1920 to 83·82 feet in 1921. The *White Heather*, owned by Sir Charles Allom, did not carry so much sail as Lord Waring sets upon her to-day, but she had a Marconi topmast and was a very smart cutter. The *Nyria* was regarded as a nippy little boat, and her enterprizing owner, Mrs. Workman, had given Mr. Charles Nicholson, her designer, a free hand to rig the boat as he liked. Charlie Nicholson, always in advance of the current opinion scientifically, had rigged *Nyria* with an enormous Bermudian mainsail. This was the first Bermudian mainsail ever set upon a first-class cutter. The *Britannia*'s opponents were thus thoroughly up-to-date vessels. The King came down to Southend on Thursday evening and slept on board the *Victoria and Albert,* which was anchored off the long pier at Southend-on-Sea. On Friday morning it blew great guns, and over the triangular course round the Nore, West Oaze buoy, and the Mouse Lightship the *Britannia* overpowered her two opponents and won the race.

The next day was the remarkable light weather race which we call 'Down Swin', namely from Southend to Harwich. There was an absolute flat calm off the pier. His Majesty came on board, and scores of motor-boats and rowing boats gathered about us laden with trippers and sight-seers; the pierhead was black with people. It was so calm that we all lay at our kedges. The reader can picture now the three great yachts holding to their anchors, a perfect cloud of canvas, everything set, and the last drain of the flood-tide just lapping their bows. They were completely surrounded by small boats almost touching their sides, the gay and good-natured folk from East London seeming to have every kind of musical instrument. So we all lay for an hour in the blazing heat of the July sun.

I have sailed the old Southend to Harwich match 'Down Swin' a great many times, and in many different yachts in all sorts of weather. I am fully aware that it is the fashion nowdays amongst modern yachting people to decry these East Coast races and the races on the estuary of the Thames, but I disagree with them. The fashionable folk think there is no place like the Solent. Scottish yachtsmen, who certainly know good racing when they see it, do not like the sandy tidal shallows of the Thames Estuary. 'Ocean Racing' yachtsmen, who in recent years have sailed one or two races in a season from Cowes round the Fastnet Rock to Plymouth, no doubt regard the races in the Thames Estuary as about equal to the Serpentine or Round Pond. But I have sailed some forty races a year for more than thirty years (omitting the War) on every part of the coast, and have often made a thousand miles of passages besides, and I declare there are few better courses than 'Down Swin' and 'Up Swin'. I sailed from Southend to Harwich once in the 20-Rater *Senga*, a miserable type of craft compared with a modern 12-Metre or 15-Metre. She had no cabin accommodation, the owner had forgotten our drink, and our sandwiches fell into the bilge water, of which the *Senga* had plenty, for her decks leaked and it blew hard and rained incessantly. What a race it was! A tremendous tussle for 50 miles in wind and sea! Charlie Bevis was our skipper and Sycamore came as pilot, so we were handled well and won the match. After we passed the Maplin Spit, there was the devil's own short sea running in the South-west Reach, and the 'Twenties' were throwing such a dust, you could not see for spray. A 2,000-ton steamer lying at her anchor in the Great Nore Channel that day broke her cable. Below Southend it is not always as quiet as the Round Pond, it can do funny things in the Thames Estuary.

But this is by the way. The race I am spinning my yarn about was a calm, quiet race, a day of paltry airs. It was not *Britannia*'s weather at all. How could she win against the *White Heather* and *Nyria*? On Friday, 15 July 1921, the previous day, I had also had the honour of sailing with the King over the triangular course I have mentioned. That race was 37 miles, and that was *Britannia*'s weather. She beat the *White Heather* by ten minutes, and the Bermudian-rigged *Nyria* by 14 minutes. The presence of the King on board his own yacht in the River Thames in a sailing-match had only occurred once previously in history, when Charles II sailed one of his yachts from Greenwich to Gravesend and back against another owned by his brother James, Duke of York. Now on the Saturday, 16th July, the wind had all gone, and I confess I expected to see the *Nyria* ghost away from us. As the ebb began to come, the three yachts crept slowly past the Shoebury Sands and left Southend in a dim heat haze astern. Major Hunloke was careful and patient and the crew keen and alert. Three miles below Southend the *Britannia* was showing her bowsprit ahead of the *Nyria*. The *White Heather* was not a hundred yards astern. Off the Blacktail Spit, abreast of the Mouse Lightship at two o'clock, the ebb had come pretty strong, and with a nice light breeze the *Britannia* held her position, and, surely gaining, was three minutes ahead at the Maplin Light. Only a little more than a cable's length it seemed in distance. The other two yachts were overlapping. Through the South-west Reach, and past the Swin Middle to the shallow point where you enter the East Swin there were light airs ahead and abeam. We were so close to the *Nyria* and *White Heather* off the Gunfleet that the King several times conversed with those aboard the other yachts across the calm water. I think it was about abreast of the Gunfleet Light, if my memory is correct, that, although the *Nyria* had drawn a little out on our weather, a faint breeze seemed to tell upon our jackyard topsail, and it did not take the top of the *Nyria*'s triangular sail. So from the lee berth did the *Britannia* steadily but surely draw out a commanding lead. The wind freshened until the old ship began to rustle the water and leave a slight white track upon the sparkling diamonds of the sea astern, and we were soon a quarter of a mile ahead of the *Nyria*. The *White Heather* was striving hard to catch the Bermudian, and the *Britannia* was now obviously gaining upon the newer yachts. So they entered that broad lower part of the East Swin, which is appropriately called the King's Channel. His Majesty himself took the wheel, and no sooner had he done so than a jolly breeze piped up. We reached through the King's Channel in a noble procession at high speed. There were no less than five admirals sailing in the *Britannia* that day, and I remember that when he was steering, the King, more by way of a joke than anything else, told them all to lie flat on the deck with their heads below the weather rail, and down they all went like yachtsmen should. At this moment it was a thrilling spectacle. Gazing aloft the whole contour of *Britannia*'s sail-plan was an absolutely perfect sight to the eye of the yachtsman . . . a perfect mainsail, the seam of each cloth tracing from luff to leech a perfect parabolic curve, the jackyard-topsail, headsails and working jib topsail without a tremble. Her gunwale not quite awash, but the vessel nicely heeled, sheets perfectly trimmed, and the crew with heads below the weather bulwarks all flat upon the deck, the sleek black hull with bow just lifting to the waves, leaving her glistening track in the sun, and alone standing at his wheel the King. His Majesty, being dressed all in white, could be clearly seen by many yachts and craft passing along the broad highway from the eastern coast to the Thames, and many a cheer was raised on that summer's afternoon for the *Britannia*. We thundered along from the West Rocks to the Cork, but again it lightened towards the evening. The fast cutter *White Heather* passed the *Nyria* as they reached merrily along the Gunfleet, but on all points the *Britannia* increased her lead that day and won the race; indeed, she was a mile and a half ahead when we made Harwich.

	H.	M.	S.
Britannia (winner)	6	15	16
White Heather (second prize) ..	6	26	54
Nyria	6	32	38

B. Heckstall-Smith: *The Britannia and her Contemporaries.* 1929

Candida leads Cambria, Astra, and Westward

'ALL COMPETITORS had trouble with their spinnakers.' This laconic comment often appeared in the accounts of racing in J Class days—and its brevity shows how such incidents were accepted. Yet to us, the struggle of a dozen men with a boom as thick as their chests and long, like the boat itself, supported by a monster spinnaker of uncertain reactions, deserves no such easy dismissal.

These boats travelled fast and soon overhauled the Beken launch. In the second photograph *Candida* has gone by, but the tan-sailed yacht seen astern of *Cambria* hasn't travelled far between the two shots.

Cambria and *Astra* were two of the new J Class boats whose building marked the new departure in the 'big class' which the rule inaugurated. The photographs were taken in 1930, off Cowes and the Prince Consort buoy, still used by today's racing boats.

A Race aboard Shamrock—1927

ONE DAY, when we were all racing during Cowes Week, I was myself sailing in *Shamrock*; the wind was variable and fluky, and we were leading. The sky became very overcast, and we were turning to windward back from Ryde to Cowes to finish the race. Along the south-east edge of the Brambles the wind increased to a pretty hot puff, and the *Britannia* completely outpointed and outsailed the *Shamrock*, and passed high on our weather in a way I had never seen her do before in that weight of wind. All of us—*Britannia, Lulworth, Shamrock* and *White Heather*—had every stitch of light weather canvas set: our big jackyarders and working jib-topsails. A noble company. The King was on board *Britannia*. Sir Mortimer Singer now had bought the *Lulworth*, a somewhat unlucky big cutter, built by the late Mr. Lee in 1920 and called the *Terpsichore*, and afterwards re-christened the *Lulworth* by Mr. Weld, of Lulworth Castle, who sold her to Sir Mortimer. The *Lulworth* was sailing remarkably well, but the *Britannia* still better. Lord Waring was aboard his *White Heather*, and Colonel Neill and I were in *Shamrock*, and old Sycamore at our wheel. And here, indeed, was a company of noble cutters, even as grand as the old fleet *Navahoe, Valkyrie, Satanita,* and *Calluna,* which the *Britannia* had led into Cowes Roads when I was but a boy of twenty-three years old in 1893.

Now today, in 1927, here is *Britannia* leading the fleet into Cowes Roads again. I remember thinking as the black hull of the upstanding *Britannia* walked past us hand-over-fist between Ryde Middle and the easternmost yachts moored in Cowes Roads, 'This is a wonderful thing.' Duncan Neill, my old friend, said to me, 'Bookstall,' for such is my nickname by some 'the old *Britannia* is the best of the bunch yet, they can say what they like.'

Then a deuce of a squall hit us, crashed upon us out of Cowes Roads, when three of us were laying across from the Brambles to Old Castle Point on the starboard tack. *Britannia* leading, and *Lulworth* and *Shamrock* close together. Lord Waring's yacht I could not see, but *White Heather* was fizzing along on the port tack somewhere under Norris Castle. The sea was lashed into a white mist of spindrift, and the *Shamrock* lay down to her skylights. I never saw a yacht more flat. It was one of the hottest and most sudden squalls I remember on a summer's day. We could do nothing. We could not even get the jib-topsail off her for several minutes. But the *Shamrock*, 23-Metres, is a mighty good boat. She was no chicken then, nineteen years old. She was flat on her side, but was still manageable, and old Sycamore was full of heart and confidence. He said to me, 'Can you see the others? I suppose it's the same for all.' He was kneeling at his wheel, and seemed right down in the water, so I climbed up to the weather rail and 'took a look at the others.' *Lulworth* was rattling and snorting like a horse, she was being jilled, the water streaming from her scuppers. The *Britannia* was obviously out of hand. Caught in this way with the big sailplan, they had let her luff too heavy, and she had borne away suddenly and heeled to a great angle, flooded her decks, and come-to again, but she was going faster than *Lulworth*. As I watched her for a minute or so, I could see Sir Philip Hunloke and a helper with him on her wheel, and the King by them. They soon got her going again, and the *Britannia* tacked to port in Cowes Roads and came thundering through the line of the Royal Yacht Squadron the winner of the match. The *Lulworth* was second and the *Shamrock* third, closely followed by *White Heather*.

B. Heckstall-Smith: *The Britannia and her Contemporaries.* 1929

A Beken Puzzle

THESE two practically identical photographs present a puzzle. The identifications on the plates say *Shamrock* and *Shamrock V*. But is that true? It's certain they're not the same boat and we are certain that they aren't *Shamrocks*. Apart from rigging and sail differences one can spot variations in the deck plan, the superstructure — and even the life rings. The photographs were taken on the same day in August 1934. When it comes to *Shamrocks*, neither could have been *Shamrock IV* of the 1920 Challenge because she had already been broken up, while *Shamrock III* had fought for the Cup in 1903 — thirty-one years before the camera shutter clicked to take these two pictures. Both Keith Beken and his father, the famous Frank, were as puzzled as ourselves; they were both sure that the yachts are not *Astra* and *Candida*, just as we feel that neither boat is a *Shamrock*. The puzzle remains for a reader to solve. Nevertheless our sneaking suspicion is that the top yacht is *Britannia* and the bottom one *Astra* or *Velsheda*.

*On the two preceding pages is one of those sights
about which Heckstall-Smith wrote with such
emotion. Even though the breeze is on the light side,
these yachts are travelling at a respectable pace and
Britannia, who has obviously picked up a puff, is
frolicking along with a bone in her teeth.*

*Once again one is surprised by the closeness to
each other that these giants were accustomed to sail
when racing. Spare a thought for the helmsmen and
crews when rounding a mark with 100 tons of
superb vessel at 12 or 15 knots, snapping at the
heels of another or being snapped themselves.*

*Those who have witnessed such moments are
lucky indeed. They are not likely to be seen again.*
(PAGES 68–9)

Shamrock V and the America's Cup

In the 1930 America's Cup challenge, *Shamrock* was worked entirely by the strong arms of her crew, as you can see in the fold-out photograph. Harold Vanderbilt, however, had filled the defender *Enterprise* with gadgets and winches, each one more ingenious than the last. Indeed, a large part of his crew saw nothing of any race as they were below, industriously winding handles. As a result, and in an effort to curb the drift towards 'mechanization', it was finally decided that all mechanical apparatus would have to be sited on deck—which robbed things of much of their interest! But in the interval, *Shamrock* had been sent packing by four victories to none.

After such a trouncing, and with the death of Sir Thomas Lipton in 1931, one might have thought that *Shamrock*'s career was at an end. However, she passed into the hands of the redoubtable T. O. M. Sopwith and went on to dominate the 'Big Class' in the 1932 season. The photograph on the following two pages shows her in her usual position in English waters—at the head of the fleet. Behind her we can recognize the glorious old *Britannia*—she was built in 1893! Following *Britannia* is *Velsheda*, and, probably, *Astra*, of both of which more later. But here, *Shamrock*'s position in the race as she remorselessly covers her pursuers is one of great strength.

(PAGES 71–4 AND 76–7)

A Tacking Match between Shamrock IV and Britannia

THE RACE between *Britannia* and *Shamrock* on 12 June 1928, was from Harwich to Southend, and we did not sail up the Swin, but farther south, up the Barrow Deeps. Picture it for a moment, smooth water and a light wind from the west. This means a turn to windward for thirty or forty miles . . . .

The yachtsmen of the joint clubs of Southend gave the prize, and the Royal Harwich Yacht Club people started us outside Harwich Harbour off the Platters buoy at eleven o'clock. The length of the course was 48 miles, and we reached the finish off Southend Pier at 4.30 p.m. A more perfect day for yacht-racing could not be imagined, sunny clear weather, a blue sky and fleecy white clouds, a delightful topsail breeze. The *Britannia* had to allow 1 minute 12 seconds to the two gaff-rigged cutters, *Shamrock* and *White Heather*, and 4 minutes 14 seconds to the new Bermudian-rigged cutter *Cambria*. The latter yacht was William Fife's most recent addition to the racing fleet. She had won her first race on the opening day of the season at Harwich, beating the *Britannia* and *Shamrock* handsomely in half a gale of summer wind, but so far as I could judge the new Bermudian was distinctly under-canvassed for light or ordinary weather. For the new vessel, however, which was 12 feet shorter than *Britannia*, to sail all round a triangular course ahead of the old cutter and finish ahead of her in '*Britannia*'s weather' was a great triumph. *Cambria,* as the season's racing of 1928 afterwards proved, had insufficient sail area for light winds. The interest taken by yachtsmen in the opening races of the season of 1928 was intense. The questions people were asking were: How will the new Bermudian-rigged yachts *Astra* and *Cambria* sail against the gaff-rigged cutters? Will they beat the *Shamrock* and *White Heather*? Will the King's old cutter *Britannia* be completely out-classed? On 12th June there was a right good breeze, the Thames Estuary was as smooth as I have ever known it, with such a smart breeze from south-west to south, and its wide shallows and deep channels were very attractive. The start was before the wind with main-booms squared off to port, and the breeze on the starboard quarter, the starting-line was between the big steam yacht *Sona,* belonging to Sir William Berry, and the Platters buoy. Old Captain Sycamore made a beautiful start in the *Shamrock.* He was extremely clever in picking his position about a minute before the starting-gun. He took up a leeward position and

then reached up from the leeward end of the line with plenty of way. He was sufficiently wide of the three other yachts to avoid being blanketed, and as the starting-gun fired he bore up through the line exactly with the flash of it. The *White Heather* drew into the track of *Shamrock*'s wake. The *Britannia* was upon the *White Heather*'s weather quarter, and the *Cambria* last and farthest to windward. The start, notwithstanding the length of the race, turned out to be of vital importance. From the Platters buoy to the Cork Lightship is less than 2 miles. It was soon noticeable that we in the *Britannia* had to run too dead for the Cork to do much good. The more leeward boats, having the breeze more quarterly, gathered more speed than *Britannia,* The most windward boat, *Cambria,* the Bermudian, was the deadest before the wind, and she dropped astern. The four vessels thus luffed round the Cork Lightship, leaving it to starboard in this order: *Shamrock, White Heather, Britannia, Cambria.* Directly they rounded the lightship, where they now turned their course to starboard towards the Thames Estuary, sheets were trimmed, and they were laid on a close reach on the starboard tack. There was a smart breeze, and the speed about 10 knots. They laid an almost straight line from the Cork Lightship past the Cork Sand buoy to the West Rocks. This was a clean, close-hauled leg of nearly 6 miles, and a pretty good test of speed. The *Britannia* luffed out a couple of hundred yards wide on to the *White Heather*'s weather quarter. I think her speed just at that moment must have been rather unexpected by Captain Mountefield, the skipper of *White Heather,* because he did not luff at all to keep *Britannia* in his wake. I know I was astonished by the speed of the old ship as we stood off for the Cork Sand. The *Britannia* sailed clean past the *White Heather,* and gave her a pretty good shaking, and it shivered her sails so that the *Cambria* reached past the *White Heather* also. The *Britannia* now came up on the weather quarter of *Shamrock,* but she never got on terms with her. Sycamore never let her come wide, but now and then drew his luff and watched us most carefully. It was about 8 miles from our start off Felixstowe sea-front to the West Rock buoy, and we did it in just 50 minutes. At the buoy I timed the four boats: *Shamrock* 11. 50. 0; *Britannia,* 11. 50. 40; *Cambria,* 11. 52. 15; *White Heather* 11. 53. 0. Now we trimmed our main-sheets for a dead peg to windward, and it was evident we were in for a great close-hauled race. Two good long tacks were made to fetch the north-east end of the Gunfleet, and then the yachts entered the broad King's Channel, or East Swin, at 12.10 p.m., with the ebb-tide getting slack. For more than thirty years I had not seen such a glorious set-to of cross-tacking as now took place between the big cutters along the Gunfleet. There were miles to go to windward, smooth water, a smart breeze, a glinting sunlit sea. Yacht-racing was revived at last! I had seen such things in my youth in 1893 and 1894, when *Britannia* and her first rivals were built, but not since. The *Shamrock* must have weather-bowed the *Britannia* a dozen times. Can I sketch the race as it passes now for the long miles up to the channel of the Barrow Deeps? The *Shamrock* about a hundred yards ahead of the *Britannia*. On these rivals centres the seaman's interest; the *White Heather* and the *Cambria* fighting a great battle too, worked farther easterly, and perhaps with less wind dropped astern. Folks forget all about 'time allowances and square roots, and such ritual' when they are in the heat of a great race, and all is a-blowing and a-going. Can the *Britannia* pass the *Shamrock*? If she can do so, she will win this match from Harwich to Southend. On the starboard tack, standing off the Gunfleet, *Britannia* is 150 yards astern and on the *Shamrock*'s weather quarter; gradually foot by foot *Britannia* creeps up, sailing faster, until she gets within 100 yards or even 80 yards of *Shamrock*; then she strikes the 'back wind' of *Shamrock*'s sails — the 'back wind' which disturbs the 'vacuum' of our mainsail, about which clever theorists have so much to say and love to talk. But sure enough here is proof, and it is true that every time the *Britannia* gets within this distance — about 80 or 100 yards — her life deadens, she sails perceptibly slower, and drops back until 200 yards again separates the vessels. Then, having fallen back that distance, she recovers her speed and begins to creep up to the *Shamrock* again. Not once or twice, but twenty times in exactly the same manner this occurred in the race from Harwich to Southend. What is to be done? *Britannia* will never pass the *Shamrock* that way. So Sir Philip Hunloke spins his wheel and slaps her round on to the port tack. Captain Sycamore, watching him like a cat would a mouse, slaps *Shamrock* round too, and again he holds *Britannia* on the new tack just as surely as he held her before. Now we are on the port tack, standing towards the Gunfleet Sand, so our helmsman tries ramping her a bit full to endeavour to get through *Shamrock*'s lee, the *Britannia* eats her way ahead inch by inch with wind clear, but alas! what she gains in 'distance ahead' she loses in 'distance to leeward'; so as they tack again the position is unchanged. Try some other gambit. Sir Philip now tries two very short tacks — tack and tack again within a hundred yards — this is a rare scramble for the crew, all a-hauling on the head-sheets and backstays. Sycamore makes exactly the same manœuvres as his opponent, and twice weather-bows the King's yacht with all the severity possible. So again it is 'fifty-fifty', but all the time *Shamrock* holds her advantage. Thus for an hour the battle goes on, helmsmen equally skilful, the professional and the amateur, nothing to chose between them, and the crews of the yachts perfectly matched working with all their energy at the sheets until their hands are sore. One humorous incident. *Britannia*, trying one of these sudden short tacks in attempting to take *Shamrock* by surprise, got one of her preventer backstays jammed, and Sir Philip had to throw her up head to wind to get it clear. Sycamore and Colonel Duncan Neill, ready for any of the old tricks of the game, thought the *Britannia* was playing them a 'false tack' — that is, to pretend to throw a tack half-round, and to swing back to the same tack as before. If this can be done successfully the leading boat may find herself on the opposite tack to her opponent, and so let her slip away. But it was no false tack *Britannia* was trying, her weather backstay was caught up, and she was thus forced to lose her way by being held head to wind. Of course *Shamrock* did not know of our trouble. What did she do? Bless you! they put her head to wind also, to 'wait and see' which tack *Britannia* was going to fill upon, so that they could make dead certain upon which tack to fill the *Shamrock* and take our wind as before! So there, for a few seconds, was the curious spectacle of the two great cutters both lying head to wind, with their sails rattling and shaking in the breezes, the *Shamrock* 50 yards dead ahead of the *Britannia*, waiting for one another like boxers taking a breather. The *Britannia* made a semaphore to the *Shamrock*, 'Thank you for waiting for us until we cleared our backstay'. Then they filled away again, and after trying every ingenuity of racing seamanship, they stood on the starboard tack for the Barrow Lightship, the *Shamrock* still ahead of the *Britannia*. The times at the Barrow Deep Lightship were: *Shamrock*, 1. 35. 0; *Britannia*, 1. 36. 30; *White Heather*, 1. 39. 20; *Cambria*, 1. 39. 28.

The channel called the Barrow Deeps is about 14 miles long, and it was a dead thresh to windward through two-thirds of it. Then at about 3 p.m. the wind softened in the broiling afternoon sun, and it looked as if there might be some fluking. The *Shamrock* slowly increased her lead in a long light reach. The *White Heather* came creeping up until her bowsprit was almost up to *Britannia*'s counter. The *Cambria* was not two minutes astern, but she lost some distance by having to keep away from a steamer which had a lighter or barge in tow on a long towline. At about 3.15 a thunderstorm, or, as Essex sailors say, a 'tempest', began to darken the sky over the haze of the Kentish coast, and out of this the wind began to come in hot puffs, some very fresh, sending us rattling along and cutting up a dust on a broad reach towards the West Oaze, with the breeze south-south-west and south. We had turned to windward for 30 miles, and during the whole race in 5½ hours we sailed perhaps 55 or 60 miles of water. We bore up round the West Oaze buoy: *Shamrock*, 3.47.0; *Britannia*, 3.48.52; *White Heather*, 3. 49. 14; *Cambria*, 3. 51. 11; our lee decks not two planks awash. The last leg of the long match had come, and the wind was such that every vessel was driven at full speed.

Check sheets and let 'em have the weight of it; the four yachts flying like the devil in a straight line from the West Oaze to Southend. Out of the thunder blast from the south-west came the weight of the storm. The *Britannia* in a dust of foam and the water churning about the helmsman's feet, caught the *Shamrock* in a minute and a half, and was almost overlapping her when the winning-gun fired off Southend Pier. On the time allowance, the *White Heather* beat the *Cambria* for second prize by 4 seconds and the *Britannia* by 10 seconds! This was the finish:

	H.	M.	S.
Shamrock (winner)	4	28	8
Britannia	4	28	23
White Heather	4	29	25
Cambria	4	32	31

The corrected time of the race I will record, because it is so extraordinarily close after 5½ hours' sailing:

	H.	M.	S.
Shamrock	4	26	56
White Heather	4	28	13
Cambria	4	28	17
Britannia	4	28	23

It was a race won by *Shamrock* through the splendid judgment and skill of old Sycamore, and I give him full credit, but the *Britannia* never won or lost a better sailing-match. For hour upon hour the helmsmen of *Shamrock* and *Britannia* jockeyed one another with fairness and skill that it was good to see, and along the Gunfleet they had the glory of this great race to themselves. They ended the day travelling 12 knots, separated by a length, providing the sightseers with a dramatic finish.

B. Heckstall-Smith: *The Britannia and her Contemporaries.* 1929

Velsheda

It is difficult to conjure up in the imagination a nobler or more majestic sight than *Velsheda*, proud and tall, as she runs at hull speed across our bows.

Year of build:	*1933*
LOA:	*127 ft. 3 in.*
LWL:	*83 ft.*
Beam:	*21 ft. 5 in.*
Draft:	*15 ft.*
Sail area:	*7,542 sq. ft.*
Tons TM:	*205*

Velsheda

VELSHEDA, steel-hulled to designs by Charles E. Nicholson and built in his Camper & Nicholson yard at Gosport in 1900, seems to pursue her shadow through the spray thrown up by her bow wave as she leads *Shamrock V* up the Solent. The elements have provided weather on a scale fit for these two superb vessels. Looking at *Velsheda*, framed by the clouds and a white capped sea, one understands the shared passion of owners and crews for racing in the 'Big Class'. This *was* a different world. The Big Class was big in every sense of the word. It was ruinously expensive. It was difficult and complicated and took a long time to get a J boat into action. It needed a great many men—and competent men at that. The drama of the fight took place miles out of sight—and all the Sunday afternoon crowds saw were a few moments as the great yachts came in to pick up their moorings. In fact little would be known of great moments if it hadn't been for a small launch belonging to a photographer. On this occasion Beken has caught a shaft of sunlight soon to be snuffed out by the banked up clouds and the lowering weather. It was perhaps symbolic. For the great days of the great yachts were drawing on and under clouds of canvas they were already sailing into the past.

Astra

Year of build :	1928
LOA :	115 ft.
LWL :	75 ft.
Beam :	20 ft. 2 in.
Draft	13 ft. 10 in.
Sail area :	7,507 sq. ft.
Tons TM :	164

▶

SOME yachts, like some women, inspire an all-transcending love. Such was *Astra*. Her owner, Hugh F. Paul, of the Royal Thames and many other yacht clubs, readily forgave all her faults, accepted without rancour that she was not always the fastest, passed over the wrinkles of her age and was faithful to her unto death. At 115 feet LOA *Astra* was incontestably a giant—and she competed in all the great races, was well maintained and well run. The photographs on pages 84–5 and pages 87–90 show her in her glory—and also help one understand her owner. In the prevailing fresh wind *Astra* is reefed. With a stiff leading breeze and under spinnaker she is travelling at speed. But not travelling fast enough one supposes since, as on pages 84–5, she was often led by other boats. She was certainly outclassed by *Shamrock V* for instance, who is seen ahead of her there. The latter was of course the first boat designed by Charles E. Nicholson to the Universal Rule, which a short time before had been adopted for the Big Boats—now to be called the J Class.

Astra on the other hand had been designed by the same Charles Nicholson to the International Rule and was slightly smaller all round.

(PAGES 84–5 AND 87–90)

Astra and Velsheda

THIS LOVELY yacht with her wings outspread is *Astra*. The man for whom she was built kept her for nineteen years—right up to his death.

Velsheda (pages 92–3) reaches along in a handsome breeze. The sun shines, the deck is dry and most of the crew get a short spell of relaxation. Aboard *Astra* in the second photograph (pages 94–5) it is a different story. Hard on the wind the deck is covered with spray. She is heeled so that it is almost impossible to stand upright. Her lee rail is under water. The helmsman is bent over the wheel. The low bulwarks and absence of lifelines augmented tacking risks. 'Man overboard' was a frequent cry in those days and such accidents in our cold waters were often enough fatal, simply because in the fisherman tradition these hardy crewmen were generally bad swimmers.

(*Velsheda*, PAGES 92–3)
(*Astra*, PAGES 94–5)

Sir Thomas Lipton and Shamrock V

TEN YEARS had passed since Sir Thomas Lipton had convinced himself that he could win the America's Cup—and now he was to throw down yet another gauntlet. He was over 80 years old and this had to be the last assault—and many Americans would have liked to see him win. Once more the routine was set in motion (it practically knew its way home in the dark by now). There was the exchange of letters—carbon copies of previous correspondence would have done perfectly well—the architects got down to their drawing-boards and then the builders set to work. To repel the one English boat the Americans built four. *Enterprise*, winner of the American defence selection trials, pulverized the challenger. Nobody had asked for such an overwhelming victory and all felt sorry for Sir Thomas who followed the races without comment aboard his motor-yacht *Erin* (he was never to set foot on *Shamrock V*).

The sequel to these events had all the trappings of a typically British paradox. On his return from his fifth and possibly most abortive attempt to regain the Cup—the goal of a lifetime—Lipton saw himself elected a member of the Royal Yacht Squadron, the club which had consistently refused him entry. Successful, enjoying royal friendship, knighted by his King, he had been cold-shouldered as a 'tradesman', a man of business and humble birth. Lipton accepted the honour done to him—but died the following year without ever once having set foot in his new club.

Endeavour and Britannia

importunate strangers. On the left in this photograph are Sir Thomas and Lady Sopwith. Sopwith was an aeroplane builder who applied some of the principles of aerodynamics to the two challengers which he built in the quest for the America's Cup. His first *Endeavour*, designed by Charles E. Nicholson, got closer to getting 'that old mug' back to the European side of the Atlantic than any yacht before or since.

In the facing photograph *Endeavour*, to the leeward of the grand old *Britannia*, appears to point higher—and to travel faster, if that bow wave is anything to go by. Here's a good breeze—but the leaden skies betray the fact that this picture was taken off the south coast of England. Perhaps this picture also goes a little way to explaining the repeated successes of the United States defence of the America's Cup.

British designers, builders and sailmakers alike all know without any shadow of doubt that at all costs they should produce a light weather boat. They knew all this well enough but crew training and boat tuning were things that they couldn't control. Worse than this, 'skinned out' masts threatened the heads of the crew, and light weather sails such as 'drifters' and 'ballooners' arrived at Newport without having been tried out or 'tuned' in any way at all. It doesn't surprise one in these circumstances to learn that *Endeavour*, despite meticulous preparation, ran off her first three races with a light genoa borrowed from one of the short-listed and eliminated possible defenders, *Vanitie*.

THE STRIPPED out, hard-lying accommodation of the big racing yacht could be turned over to the other side of the coin — the comfortable motor yacht aboard which one could live and receive one's guests in peace and quiet, remote from

Endeavour II

Endeavour II — the English hope. With *Endeavour* T. O. M. Sopwith was the owner of the fastest and most advanced yacht in the world and had been within a touch of regaining the America's Cup. It was to be a brief moment of truth. *Endeavour II*, faster still, should win. See how she leads the rest of the Big Boats. Once again there's a fresh breeze and that one mast has to support the conflicting loads of a tremendous press of sail. In this photograph it seems that the better part of the crew is mobilized to strong-arm the spinnaker. But in spite of *Endeavour II*'s significant design advance over *Endeavour,* by the time she came to the killing ground off Newport, Rhode Island, in 1937, the American defence had passed into the hands of a new, young design genius, Olin Stephens, and an even faster American yacht, *Ranger.* Once again the British were back behind the Eight Ball. *Endeavour II* was a splendid steel-built cutter, designed by Charles E. Nicholson and built at the Camper & Nicholson yard at Gosport in 1936 — and, as witness of a passing age, *Ranger* and *Endeavour II* were the last J boats ever to be built.

Year of build:	*1936*
LOA:	*135 ft. 10 in.*
LWL:	*86 ft. 7 in.*
Beam:	*21 ft. 7 in.*
Draft:	*15 ft.*
Sail area:	*7,546 sq. ft.*
Tons TM:	*228*

Endeavour

Sometimes beneath a marvellous Beken photograph any caption would seem ordinary. Such is the case here. *Endeavour* was simply the marvellous racing machine that she is seen to be in this picture.

Yankee in English Waters

Year of build: 1930
LOA: 126 ft.
LWL: 86 ft. 3 in.
Beam: ——
Draft: 15 ft.
Sail area: 7,220 sq. ft.
Tons TM: 228

THE photographs on the facing page and on the following two pages (where *Yankee* leads *Candida*) can be dated without any shadow of doubt as Beken vintage 1935. This was the year that *Yankee* came to England—for a season's racing in the Big Class which was to be a particularly brilliant one. The course of affairs was running pretty fast in the world as a whole. This was paralled in yachting and the main stream of development was in the end to bring *Yankee* the fullest of careers. She first came on the scene in 1930. Designed by Frank Paine for the J. S. Lawrence Syndicate, *Yankee* was one of the quartet of yachts built to fight off the *Shamrock V* challenge—the first America's Cup series to be contested in the J Class. She was a good boat which could carry her canvas in a breeze and which put up some notable performances: 30 miles in 2 hours 47 minutes 59 seconds and, on another occasion, 10 miles on the wind at 13·25 knots. But this undoubted 'power' had to be paid for in terms of sluggish performance in light airs. It was no surprise therefore that her rival *Enterprise* was the preferred defender. In 1933 Sopwith and *Endeavour* took up Lipton's quest, the latter having died two years before. *Yankee* was modified by her designer, particularly in her forebody, and actually dominated the elimination trials. However, looking back it is evident that the American selection committee had prolonged these deliberately to make it possible for another possible defender, *Rainbow*, campaigned by Vanderbilt, to be progressively improved. As the final eliminating races got under way *Yankee* was an odds-on favourite to defend the Cup. But over four races she managed to drop two owing to sustaining damage; a broken spreader on the first occasion and a torn genoa on the other. The choice fell on *Rainbow* but her owner was soon to be in a very hot seat indeed. The first two Cup races were victories for *Endeavour*. Vanderbilt straightaway invited Frank Paine to join the defence team and to bring his best spinnakers with him. . . .

But there were golden days yet to come for *Yankee*. Gerald Lambert bought her and in 1935 she came to Cowes for the 'Big Cutter' regattas, and this is where the Beken camera 'shot' her. In 1937 she was again altered by her owner and designer in order to take part in eliminators for a new Cup defence, destined to be the last sight of the Js in the America's Cup story: *Ranger* v. *Endeavour II*. *Yankee*'s modifications stopped her dead! All concerned hurried back to the 1936 rig and with this *Yankee* took part in the traditional New York Club Cruise, in company with the two *Endeavours* from Britain and her own compatriots *Rainbow* and *Ranger*. The result of this series of passage races is interesting. *Ranger* exhibited a crushing superiority with twelve first guns and one second; *Yankee* scored one first and one second; *Endeavour II* chalked up seven seconds, and *Rainbow* four. These results seem to confirm the outcome of the Cup series itself.

(PAGES 110—111: *Candida* AND *Yankee*)

Britannia and the Evolution of the Big Yachts

BRITANNIA retired from racing in 1897, and, except for a few days in August 1899, she was not heard of again as a racing yacht until 1913. It is rather strange that in so long a lapse of time her type and form should not have become so out-of-date as to be altogether useless for racing purposes. For sixteen years we had forgotten her.

In the years 1913 and 1914 King George raced her, and then came the War. It was not until the seasons of 1920 and 1921, when yacht-racing was reopened, that *Britannia* began her second career of serious racing, and met in the course of her races the yachts of more modern type against which she could really test her speed. My readers will therefore realize that the lapse of time between *Britannia*'s original career as a racing yacht and the beginning of her second racing career was in fact, twenty-three or twenty-four years. From 1897 to 1920–1. The reason why the *Britannia,* a champion first-class cutter built thirty-six years ago, is able to race with first-class cutters to-day is not because there have been no improvements, alterations, and experiments in the type of racing yachts and their design during that long period. On the contrary, many experiments have been tried, great improvements have been made, and the number of alterations has been enormous. The changes, however, since 1897 have proceeded in a curious cycle. For a number of years the cycle of the sport and the trend of racing-yacht architecture took a definite direction away from what I may call the 'Britannia idea'.

Then, after a lapse of years, that cycle took a different direction. Slowly but surely its new direction led us back towards the 'Britannia idea'.

Thus we find to-day, thirty-six years after the *Britannia* was built, the old vessel is again in the hunt. Once more she represents a very sound and satisfactory expression of the modern conception of the ideal racing yacht.

I do not for one moment wish to exaggerate the capabilities of the *Britannia* as compared with the latest productions of our skilled designers of the present day. Rating for rating the newest boats can beat the *Britannia* most days of the week. They cannot, however, do so by much. The latest productions, owing to the increase of knowledge of our leading naval architects, can develop higher speed for their immersed length than *Britannia*. They can do so on a plain reach.

In smooth water they can do so even to windward. They are faster owing to being able to be handled with lighter gear, and their hull form, with less wetted surface or frictional surface, will gather speed more quickly in light and moderate wind. But on the whole the 'improvement' which the most modern productions can claim is not very great, although I am sure there is not the least doubt it is definite.

The advantage, however, is not wholly on the side of the newest yachts. On certain heavy, dirty, rough days, which occur occasionally during an English racing summer, the more stalwart gear of the *Britannia* gives her an advantage over the new vessels. In heavy weather the new British Bermudian-rigged cutters, however, are not to be despised. As long as their stuff stands, in hard weather, rating for rating, they can beat *Britannia*. Their stuff does not always stand. *Britannia*'s stuff stands grandly. . . .

The type or form of the hull of a racing yacht has also to a great extent reverted to *Britannia*'s form. . . . The cutter *Meteor,* built in 1896 for the German Emperor, at once shows the tendency of the cycle to depart from the wholesome section of the *Britannia*. The draught of water is greatly increased, the curve of the turn of the bilge is harder. In 1897, when the smaller cutter-yacht *Bona* was built with the object of beating the *Meteor* by taking advantage of time allowance, a different section was tried, but in 1900, when the rules made it possible to build an enormous yawl, the *Sybarita,* it will be seen that the hollowness of the midship section was again exaggeration.

To beat the *Sybarita* it only became necessary to still further hollow this curve of the transverse section, to still further deepen the keel and reduce its thickness, and to place the lead upon the bottom of the keel in the form of a bulb. This was never actually attempted in any British yacht of *Britannia*'s size because the truth of the story was too obvious, and the waste of money in building an enormous vessel of that extreme type was too great, but it was done successfully in many smaller yachts. It was accomplished by Nathaniel Herreshoff in America in 1903 with the *Reliance,* which beat the *Shamrock III* in the race for the America's Cup in that year.

In the American yacht *Reliance* the cycle had departed from the *Britannia*'s type to the greatest extreme known in the history of yachting.

The *Britannia* with her LWL of 88 feet in 1893 and 90-foot main-boom had 10,300 square feet of sail and a crew of 30 men.

The cutter *Reliance* with a LWL of 89·6 feet in 1903 had a main-boom of 116 feet; she carried 16,200 square feet of sail and had a crew of 64 men.

B. Heckstall-Smith: *The Britannia and her Contemporaries.* 1929

BRITANNIA. Year of build: 1893. LOA: 122 ft. LWL: 88 ft. Beam: 23 ft. 4 in. Draft: 15 ft. Sail area: 9,235 sq. ft. Tons TM: 221.

The Universal Rule

IN ABOUT the year 1902 the New York Yacht Club determined to make up a rule which would develop a more desirable type of yacht than had been developed under the Seawanhaka and other various LWL rules, so they formed a committee to investigate the matter. One of the first moves of this committee was to send letters to the most prominent yacht designers in Great Britain, Australia, Canada, Denmark, France, Germany, Norway, Sweden and the United States asking for suggestions or formulas which in these designers' opinions would develop a wholesome type of yacht. The response was voluminous, but the committee adopted the rule suggested by N. G. Herreshoff which in its first simple formula was length multiplied by the square root of sail area, divided by the cube root of displacement. This rule, in my father's mind, was to play displacement, or room below the waterline, against sail area or driving power. You see, the cube root of displacement was the divisor, so if the displacement were large the rating would be small. But to bring the result of these measurements to a figure to be used for R, or rating, it was necessary to divide this sum by a constant. That was done by using eighteen per cent of the product, so the rule could be expressed in a

formula as $R = 0.18 \dfrac{L \times \sqrt{SA.}}{\sqrt[3]{D}}$

By about 1906 this rule was adopted by most of the larger yacht clubs in the United States and was called the Universal Rule, so that it was in general use over here before the International Yacht Racing Union was even formed and antedates the International or Metre boats by several years. It is no exaggeration to say that with the adoption of the Universal Rule the type of yacht built was a vast improvement, and I am quite sure the sailor will join me in saying they were finer than any others ever built anywhere under any rules. . . .

As time went on the Wise Men of the Club added many limits and restrictions to the Universal Rule, but as I do not want to bore the average reader we will only speak of a few of them. In about 1912 there was great interest in the P class and my father designed *Joyant*. She was nicknamed the 'Giant'. *Joyant* was of large displacement for her waterline length, so could be large all over as the cube foot of displacement was the divisor in the rule. It is my opinion that the *Joyant* was not an all round fast boat, al-

though large, but she was well sailed and so was the principal winner in her class. The success of *Joyant* made the Wise Men of the Club panicky, and as some of them had actually been connected with the yachts that *Joyant* had beaten, they made rules limiting the use of displacement as a divisor in the rule. This clause in the rule, adopted in 1913, was written up by the designer Gardner, who had designed some of the yachts beaten, and it read as follows: 'There shall be no limit on the actual displacement of yachts, but the cube root of the displacement, D as used in the measurement formula, shall never exceed twenty per cent of the LWL plus 0.50.'

At the same time there were rules written to clarify measuring length (L in the measurement), for *Joyant* and some others had been built with hollow lines at both bow and stern in the region where the so called quarter beam length measurement was taken, but these were fair easy sweeps. It is my opinion that the long bow and stern of *Joyant* made possible by hollow ends were of no benefit to her because her excessive displacement for her LWL had already limited her speed, and although I have no strong feeling about either of these additions to the rule, still I cannot help looking on them as little other than the reaction of spite by those who had been beaten. Certainly the bridging of hollow lines with an imaginary straight line, and measuring the quarter beam as if the hull were built to the straight line, is far better than the ridiculous clause in the International Rule that definitely prohibits any concaves in the hull above the water line, for this clause automatically bars the clipper bow as well as many bows and sterns most adapted to seaworthiness.

However limiting the use of displacement as a divisor in the rule has caused two important consequences. First, it has definitely ended the chances of the heavy displacement cruiser from winning races. My father did not like this at all as he had hoped some full and roomy boats, even more extreme than the New York Yacht Club 40's, would be tried. But the Wise Men of the Club were afraid that one-weather boats would be developed unless D were limited. That is, they feared types with small sail, light displacement and good length would be sure winners in a breeze while ones with large SA and large D would win in light weather. It seems the Wise Men detest one-weather yachts and say they do not make good competition, but personally I believe they are the best for yachting in the end, for with them every dog has his day even if the cats do have the night-time and the clubhouse.

The second, and perhaps the most disastrous effect that limiting D in the formula had, was to upset the whole construction of the rule, for what had before been a comparatively simple straightforward statement had now become a complex problem and the formula could be written in half a dozen ways. This of course pleased the Wise Men of the Club immensely, and such mathematicians as Norman Skene, Lane Poor and Charles Burgess have so confused and confounded the sailor that perhaps this alone will be the death knell of the Universal Rule, although without a doubt even in its present form it produces a yacht of a much more desirable type than any other rule that has been built to.

This brings us up to about the time of the *Resolute,* and I cannot resist telling about this most unfortunate yacht which the Wise Men of the Club nearly ruined, and as a consequence they nearly lost us the cup. In 1913 Lipton sent a challenge for the America's Cup through the Royal Ulster Yacht Club of Ireland. The challenge was practically unconditional and gave the challenger's waterline as 75 feet. The New York Yacht Club accepted the challenge, but as holders of the cup stipulated that 'the system of measurement, time allowance and racing rules of the N.Y.Y.C., as the same now exist, shall govern the races'. This meant the Universal Rule of measurement, so when my father was commissioned to design a trial cup defender he quite naturally turned out a yacht of 75 feet waterline which would rate low under the Universal Rule. Gardner designed the cup boat *Vanitie* of a similar waterline length, but she rated higher and as a consequence of this *Vanitie* only won nine races while *Resolute* won twenty-seven in their first two years of racing. In the meantime the challenger *Shamrock IV* had come over, and although she was only 75 feet waterline it was quite apparent from some of her proportions that she would rate very high. (I should say off-hand that she would have to allow *Resolute* nearly a quarter of an hour over the usual cup course.)

About the time of the challenger's arrival war broke out in Europe and the cup races were not held until 1920. The cup committee of the N.Y.C.C. decided now to increase the sail area of *Resolute,* strange to say, purposely to increase her rating. They feared public criticism if *Resolute* won her races by handicap while being beaten boat to boat by the challenger. But under the Universal Rule when you increase the sail area of a yacht without suitable hull increases, the rating increases more rapidly than the speed. Not only did the Wise Men of the Club butcher her nicely proportioned dimensions under the rule, but they had the Herreshoff Manufacturing Company, the builders of *Resolute,* make for *Vanitie* duplicates of the various winches and sail handling contrivances the *Resolute* had (and which the designer of *Vanitie* could not design). *Vanitie* was now almost completely redesigned from the deck up by Starling Burgess and given *Resolute*'s captain and some of her afterguard. But with all these alterations (increasing *Resolute*'s rating without increasing her speed proportionately, and increasing *Vanitie*'s speed without increasing her rating) the *Resolute* still beat *Vanitie* in 1920 in spite of these enormous handicaps, so their score of that year was *Resolute* seven firsts, *Vanitie* four firsts. The score of their first three years of racing under their gaff rigs was *Resolute* won thirty-four times while *Vanitie* won but thirteen times. I speak of this only to correct the popular opinion that *Vanitie* was the fastest yacht, but it is most likely if *Vanitie* and *Resolute* continued racing under their original proportions *Vanitie* would have won but one race out of three.

As for *Shamrock IV,* probably the *Resolute* as designed originally could have held her boat to boat and had from ten to fifteen minutes' handicap to boot. The way the Wise Men of the Club bungled up *Resolute* was a great trial to my father, who was about seventy-two years old at the time. Although he almost never used swear words, it was about then that he made the statement that he believed the world was now composed principally of three kinds of people. When asked what those three classes were, he said, 'Fools, damn fools, and sons of lady dogs.' Yes, the *Resolute* was an unfortunate and much maligned vessel. *Vanitie* did beat *Resolute* quite regularly after they were both rigged as staysail schooners and when they were rigged as leg-o'-mutton sloops, but *Vanitie* was undoubtedly handled much the best. I also credit the late good performance of *Vanitie* partly to Starling Burgess who designed her later rigs. Last impressions are often the most impressive and this has made many people think *Vanitie* a faster yacht than *Resolute,* but this was far from so the way they originally came out.

L. Francis Herreshoff: *The Common Sense of Yacht Design.* Vol. II, 1948

George Watson on Rules and Formulae

IN 1894 George Watson wrote to this effect:
Seven years ago [1887] it was much simpler to describe the form of racing yachts than it is today. At that time even cruising yachts were to some degree influenced by the old tonnage rule or its final modifications. Big or small boats they were all much of the same type. Assuming a change in scale a 'forty' might represent a 'ninety' or a 'five' with a fair measure of exactitude. If the trained eye of a qualified observer could differentiate between boats in a class, the general public could only distinguish one from another by the variation in the racing flags.

With the present day length/sail rule the variety of boat forms is enormous. Broad, narrow, deep or shoal draft, with or without centreboards, keels with reverse turned garboards, separate rudders, bulb keels — they all have their exponents and their successes. However, few of them would make much of a mark under the old rule — and few of *those* would have been able to live with the new. For this reason all study of the evolution of yacht forms will miss the point unless it takes account of and proceeds parallel with the rule of the day.

Throughout the whole history of modern yachting, measurement rules have been a headache. Looking back across the pages of journals and periodicals who forty years ago would have given only niggardly space to yachting, one can only be struck by the force of opinion which was then expressed in the columns of the *Field* and the *Yachtsman*. For one letter on this subject and another on that, one reads a dozen on the subject of the rules. Readers of those days handled their pens with the same energy as we find today in the commentating on rival theories — but more kind-heartedly than today's correspondents. They at least spared us their learned formulae. These controversies had the great merit in that they automatically preserved a great many important facts for the scrutiny of today's historians which had otherwise been lost. Even our old friend *Hunt's Magazine* in its youth was much more concerned to regale us with 'An Ode to a Yachtsman's Fiancée' or 'How Miss Delany Married a Naval Officer' than to bring us details of the rules and the conditions of the day. These must needs be culled fortuitously from the letters of irascible gentlemen arguing with each other. One must hope that the twentieth-century historian will be able to get similar profit from the controversies of our own days — and that these mathematicians who are now brandishing their rules formulae on high to the terror of all calm and tranquil yachtsmen will find a reader in the research student of 1950.

The Rule and the Boats

TO PROMOTE good racing amongst the biggest yachts it should be remembered that it is most important to insist upon the vessels being nearly the same size, but not absolutely so.

In the seasons of 1896–7 the Y.R.A. made two serious errors, firstly by permitting yachts of vastly different size to sail in the well-established class of *Britannia* and her contemporaries; secondly by altering and meddling with the Scale of Time Allowance. These errors were the beginning of the series of circumstances which eventually destroyed the British racing of the big cutters for many years.

In the year 1896 the 40-rater or 65-footer *Caress*, a boat designed by Watson, had her rating increased to 67 feet, and in this way she was allowed to start and race with the *Britannia*'s class. This was within the rules, but was most disastrous to sport. The class was open to all yachts over 65-feet rating, consequently the little *Caress*, by using a larger topsail, could increase her rating from 65 to 66 or 67, and legally demand admission to the class.

In 1896, according to the rules then in force, *Britannia*'s rating was 96·8, *Satanita*'s 99·8, *Ailsa*'s 100·1, the new cutter *Meteor* built for the German Emperor 101·9. With these yachts the *Caress* joined, being rated at 67. The *Meteor* upon a 48-mile course had to allow the *Britannia* 5 minutes 18 seconds and the *Caress* 38 minutes 19 seconds. . . .

In the season of 1896 a serious collision took place off Southsea between the German Emperor's new cutter *Meteor* and a German 20-rater designed by Herreshoff named *Isolde* (not the 40-rater *Isolde* which belonged to Peter Donaldson), owned by Baron Zedwitz. I was racing over the same course that day with the late Colonel Bagot in *Creole*, so I only saw the collision from a distance. The *Ailsa* was leading the big cutters, and the *Britannia* was just ahead of the *Meteor* at the end of the first round by the Spit Fort. The big ships were overtaking the 'Twenties', or as we called them in 1896 the '52-footers', and the *Meteor's* main-boom passed over the stern of the *Isolde,* swept the mast out of her, and completely wrecked her, killing Baron Zedwitz the owner.

This accident gave rise to a lot of discussion about the danger of sailing large cutters with long main-booms. Some said such cutters as the *Meteor* were too big to be safe, and I remember a good deal of nonsense was talked about the whole affair. The collision might have been avoided without any difficulty whatever had the Y.R.A. sailing rules been observed. However, I think the effect of this collision was partially responsible for the Y.R.A. making certain alterations in the Scale of Time Allowance in the following year which were propounded to 'discourage very large cutters from being built'.

Of course the proper way to discourage large cutters from being built was to fix a limit to the size of the yachts which would be permitted to sail in the class. This, however, was not done. What had actually occurred was this: At the end of the season of 1895, which had been productive of such wonderful sport between *Britannia* and *Ailsa*, the Y.R.A. foresaw that it might be possible to outbuild those vessels by building a yacht with less body, greater draught, and deeper keel and greater sail-carrying power. Consequently it would be possible to give that new vessel more sail area. They anticipated the designed boat of the future would be more of a 'skimming dish' than *Britannia,* and would probably beat her.

The Y.R.A. made changes in the rule of rating measurement to counteract the danger they had foreseen, but the steps they took were feeble and injurious to the existing yachts. Taking advantage of the opportunity, George Watson designed the *Meteor* for the German Emperor only one foot longer on the waterline than *Britannia,* but with 2,000 square feet more sail.

The *Meteor* had to allow the *Britannia* 6½ seconds per mile in 1896, which she could generally do in light to moderate weather, but not always in a fresh to strong wind.

In the year 1897 the Y.R.A. altered their Scale of Time Allowance, and increased the amount of time a large yacht had to give a small one, so that the German Emperor's *Meteor* had to give the Prince of Wales's cutter *Britannia* 13 seconds per mile instead of 6½ seconds. So far, then, as *Meteor* and *Britannia* were concerned for 1897, the latter was placed in an excellent position.

The position of the *Ailsa,* however, which was nearly equal in rating to the *Meteor,* was very badly affected by the changes in the time allowance. In 1895 and 1896 the *Ailsa* belonging to Mr. A. Barclay Walker had shown splendid sport racing against *Britannia,* and the lack of consideration shown to the owners of these yachts by the Y.R.A. seems to have been extraordinary.

The late Mr. Augustus Manning, speaking at a meeting of the Y.R.A. at which he presided, went so far as to say that boats the size of the *Ailsa* were 'monstrosities and undesirable'. Mr. Barclay Walker, the owner of *Ailsa,* replied in the Press in December 1896 with great truth that the British public appreciated the big class. He said that in the season of 1895 he had to allow *Britannia* 1 minute 7 seconds on a 50-mile course, but in the season of 1896, owing to the change in the rules, he had to allow her 3 minutes 23 seconds. Again owing to the addition to the time allowance scale in 1897, the *Ailsa* would have to give *Britannia* over 5 minutes. Mr. Walker pointed out that these changes made him hesitate as to whether he would race the *Ailsa* in British waters in 1897. He explained that *Britannia* and *Satanita* would suffer equally should a new yacht be built to conform to the rules in 1897, and suggested that the enormous expense which was entailed in keeping up these 'monstrosities' should receive a little more consideration from the Y.R.A.

Admiral the Hon. Victor Montagu supported Mr. Walker, and gave his opinion that the Y.R.A. were ruining what they had by taxing the existing boats, in the vain hope of improving type.

Mr. Augustus Manning replied that Mr. Walker's boat the *Ailsa,* along with *Britannia* and *Satanita,* would in the future be in a better position as regards not being outbuilt by yachts of larger rating like the *Meteor,* whilst it was not yet proved that the new rule and allowances would enable designers to beat the *Ailsa* and *Britannia* with a smaller and less costly yacht.

What Mr. Manning and his colleagues on the Y.R.A. at that time did not realize was that all future sport in the class would be destroyed by being composed of yachts of greatly different size.

The crushing addition to the time allowance was put on *above* 90 rating, and that no doubt would have the effect of preventing *Meteors* being built because *Meteor's* rating was 101·9 and *Britannia's* 96·8. But there was obviously a chance for a designer to attempt to turn out a much smaller new cutter and take many prizes.

George Watson saw this and built the *Bona* in 1897 for the Duke d'Abruzzi. Her rating was only 83·2-feet rating, and she received about 22 seconds per mile from the *Britannia* and 34 seconds per mile from the *Meteor*. . . .

Yachting people today [1929], seeing the King's yacht *Britannia* sailing so successfully in modern times, wonder why she retired from racing thirty years ago. They ask: 'Was the *Britannia* beaten?'

The reader by following these details will be able to understand why the *Britannia* became 'outclassed' and was forced to retire from racing in 1897.

In the seasons of 1893 to 1895, when the big cutter class became firmly established, it included a number of yachts which were practically the same size, and consequently the time allowance between them was negligible. It was just enough to allow any boat to change her rating and improve herself and keep going in the class, but it was not enough to spoil the sport. *Britannia*, *Valkyrie II*, *Calluna*, *Satanita*, *Navahoe*, *Vigilant*, and *Ailsa* were approximately the same rating.

The beginning of the end was when *Meteor* in 1896 came in with increased size, and when the little pot-hunter *Caress* jumped out of the 40-rating class by increasing her sail area and began to win prizes from the *bona fide* first-class yachts by means of long time allowance.

In 1897, as the result of these changes, the great class, founded by *Britannia* and her contemporaries in 1893, deteriorated and broke up. It was foolish to expect the *Britannia* and *Ailsa* to race against a small vessel like the *Bona* and give her 30 seconds per mile time allowance.

The *Satanita* was not fitted out.

The *Ailsa* raced against the *Britannia* in the Mediterranean, where the time allowance was not altered, but Mr. Barclay Walker announced that he would sail her no more in British waters. The result of the Y.R.A.'s legislation was a positive disaster. . . .

In 1907–8 the *Shamrock*, *White Heather*, and *Brynhild* began the first-class cutter-racing again. But in 1907 the Y.R.A.'s legislation went to the opposite extreme.

In the 23-Metre class of 1907–8 the rule was made that there should be no time allowance whatever. The *Brynhild* was sunk, and no other 23-Metre yacht was ever built to race upon level terms against *Shamrock* and *White Heather*.

The chance of failure—without the saving latitude of a little time allowance to permit a modicum of change in rating—was too great. Yachtsmen would not build. The 23-Metre class as a class without time allowance consisted of two boats, *Shamrock* and *White Heather*, and it expired before the 1914–18 War.

First-class cutter-racing in British waters is the most glorious, spectacular, and exhilarating of all sports.

It existed in bygone days from 1875 to 1885 between such cutters as *Kriemhilda*, *Vol-au-vent*, *Arrow*, *Cuckoo*, *Cythera*, *Formosa*, *Erycina*, *Vanduara*, *Marjorie*, *Genesta*, *Galatea*, *Samoena*, and *Irex*.

It came again in my young days between *Britannia*, *Calluna*, *Valkyrie II*, *Satanita*, *Navahoe*, *Vigilant*, *Ailsa*, and *Meteor* from 1893 to 1896.

It failed at the end of 1897.

The great sport has been re-established again by the King's example with old *Britannia*. . . .

In the present year [1929] we have first-class cutters in *Candida*, *Astra*, *Cambria*, *Shamrock* and *White Heather*. Young and old, the nucleus of a splendid class equal to the classes of the Victorian Era. I hope those who legislate for the sport of yacht-racing will be careful to preserve this new class.

Our new class of 1929 is based upon ideal principles. Our rules provide that the yachts must be of good wholesome type. As in the halcyon days of *Formosa* and *Vanduara*, or *Britannia* and *Ailsa*, our yachts are much the same size—tonnage or rating—call it what you will—but they are not necessarily exactly the same. To be too exact, or too exacting, kills sport.

B. Heckstall-Smith: *The Britannia and her Contemporaries*. 1929

The End of the Universal Rule

PERHAPS some of you are beginning to wonder why the Universal Rule went out of style if it was as desirable as described in the preceding part of this chapter [page 114]. Well, it came about somewhat as follows: During World War I some American yachtsmen were stationed in England. They seemed to have had a pretty good time of it on the whole and made the acquaintance of the yachtsmen of that country with the result that arrangements were made for small yacht racing between these countries. Most of the spade work of these arrangements was done by Paul Hammond so he should be looked upon as the father of international six-metre boat racing. It was arranged that each country was to have teams of four boats and that they would hold the races in first one country and then the other regardless of which side had won. It was further understood that they would alternate in using first the International Rule and then the Universal Rule but after the first year's racing in England under the International Rule our English cousins informed us that they were too poor to build to our rule and if we wanted to continue the racing it would have to be under the International Rule. Thus England as usual won the diplomatic victory but perhaps some day England will learn that good diplomacy, like good business, should be for the eventual good of both parties and is not only a matter of sharp practice for personal gain.

In the meantime over here the North American Yacht Racing Union had been formed and some of the most influential members of this organization had recently been beaten in the R class under the Universal Rule. (They had shown poor business judgment in having their R boats designed by firms who had not designed winners.) Well, what together with the influence of the North American Yacht Racing Union and the smaller yachts being compelled to be built to the International Rule if they wanted to race abroad, our Universal Rule went out of style, and, mind you, this happened even while men of experience on both sides of the Atlantic were nearly unanimous in calling the Universal Rule the most sensible rule in existence.

But the Universal Rule couldn't offer a king to dine with or a princess to dance with, though why any sailorman should sacrifice a handsome yacht for a homely one is hard to understand even if he had an opportunity to make a fool of himself in the presence of forty kings. And as for the princesses—well, perhaps there will never be any more handsome ones in this democratic world, certainly none who are as agreeable dancing partners as were our Universal Rule yachts. If you don't like this description of the decline and fall of the Universal Rule you can make up your own version, but you will find it won't be much more truthful.

I find that there is a great deal of confusion in the minds of young yachtsmen as to just what the Universal Rule is and just what the International Rule is, and there is little wonder, for this certainly is an age of confusion. Some people have called it the atomic age and that is a very good name indeed, for it certainly has caused confusion.

The Universal Rule is purely American. It was made by Americans for Americans and was adopted by most of the American yacht clubs, including those of Canada. Originally it was a multiple standard rule; that is, variations in amount of length, sail area and displacement changed the rating considerably, but since displacement, as used in the rule, has been limited, the rule now is basically a bi-standard rule (length and sail area) with many hull controlling limits which make it a complicated formula.

The International Rule which is pretty much a descendant of the later English Yacht Racing Association rules, is often spoken of as an addition rule, as it adds up length, breadth, girth, sail area, etc. The first of these addition rules was suggested by R. E. Froude in 1896 and called the Linear Rating Rule, for the resulting figure produced a dimension called 'linear rating' which could be used with the existing time allowance tables. In 1901 the Yacht Racing Association rule was:

$$\frac{L + B + 3/4G + 4^d + 1/2\sqrt{SA}}{2 \cdot 1} = \text{Linear Rating}$$

In 1907, when the International Yacht Racing Union finally agreed on a rule and adopted the metre as a standard of measurement, it was:

$$\frac{L + B + 1/2G + 3^d + 1/3\,S\text{-}F}{2} = \text{Rating}$$

You see it was quite similar to the English Yacht Racing Association rule. Since then there have been several changes in girth measurements and other hull or body measurements to encourage better shaped keels, etc.

The International Rule has the same limits on draft and displacement as the Universal Rule. They both measure sail area in quite similar ways, which in both cases allow lapping jibs and parachute spinnakers, or a much larger actual sail area than the measured sail area, so that both rules have become equally ridiculous in allowing large sail area to be carried on hulls which cannot be driven fast on account of having too short a waterline for the required displacement. One of the reasons there is confusion about the International Rule is because of late years several one-design classes have appeared whose sponsor, for business reasons, called them Internationals, but this misrepresentation has only taken away from the dignity of the International Rule.

L. Francis Herreshoff: *The Common Sense of Yacht Design.* Vol. II, 1948

SOVEREIGN ▶

Year of build :	1964
LOA :	69 ft. 2 in.
LWL :	45 ft. 10 in.
Beam :	12 ft. 7 in.
Draft :	8 ft. 11 in.
Sail area :	1,876 sq. ft.
Tons TM :	36

KURREWA V ▶

Year of build :	1964
LOA :	69 ft. 1 in.
LWL :	45 ft. 11 in.
Beam :	12 ft. 7 in.
Draft :	8 ft. 11 in.
Sail area :	1,876 sq. ft.
Tons TM :	36

Facing colour photograph:
The Australian 12-Metre
Kurrewa's huge spinnaker casts a green shadow on the sea. The size of boats such as these is relatively small—to an extent that the comparative size of their jibs, genoas and spinnakers transform them into 'mad' vessels whenever it blows up a bit. Helmsmen and crews have a fight on their hands to 'meet' the boat before she runs berserk. Kurrewa, renamed Levriers des Mers, is now one of the support yachts for the French assault on the America's Cup.

Colour photograph facing page 121:

Sovereign, an unsuccessful British challenger for the America's Cup, is another 12-Metre which now flies the French tricolour—she has taken up a new career as a training yacht and as such figures prominently in French plans for their first assault on the famous trophy.

Twelve Metres and the America's Cup

Majestic, rather fragile (particularly as concerns their rig), and monstrously impractical outside their terms of existence as racing machines, today's 12-Metres are nevertheless hugely satisfying to the seeker of beauty and purity of line, while for the man of research they are an ideal test bench on which to develop rig and racing sails. The traditions of the Big Boats, the great J Class, have been inherited by the Twelves — the dedication, the crew discipline, the striving for perfection, and above all the unquenchable thirst to take 'that old mug' away from the U.S.A.

Pages 122–3:
Creaming westwards up the Solent come five of the 12-Metre fleet that raced at Cowes in the years before the Second World War. K6 is the Sir Thomas Glencoat's designed and built Iris; K9 is Noresca, designed by Johan Anker of Dragon Class fame; X1 is the 1934 Fife-designed Miquette (registered in Valparaiso); K4 is a 1926 Fife design, built as Judith but launched as Modesty; and K11 is Iyruna, designed by Charles E. Nicholson and built by Camper & Nicholson in 1927.

Pages 124–5:
The David Boyd designed Sceptre, the 1958 British challenger for the America's Cup, with her Herbulot spinnaker set. The genoa is being hoisted for the next leg of the course.

The Twelve-Metres

Sceptre and Sovereign, two unsuccessful British America's Cup challengers, pictured together in the Solent.

THE Js gone, the question was to which class would the fate of the America's Cup be transferred. The solution of the experts at the outset appeared to be in a boat bigger than the 8-Metre International Rule and smaller than the 15-Metre. But in the popular view the choice could only be between the 6-Metre class—about the smallest boat that could be built to the International Rule—or the 19 and 23-Metres at the other end of the scale. In this connection, yachting's most famous historian Heckstall-Smith had one of his few comments to make on the 12-Metre class. He described them as the smallest yacht aboard which an owner of modest means could live while carrying through the regatta programme. How was it then that the 12-Metre has become the symbol of the thoroughbred racing yachts—whose periodic confrontations are inevitably thought of as battles between the giants?

Born on the eve of the First World War the International Rule came to an end for practical purposes on the eve of the succeeding War. It had suffered a heavy blow when the American-inspired Universal Rule was adopted for the America's Cup series. Essentially the deal was that the Universal Rule would look after the Big Boats while the 'little 'uns' would come under the writ of the International Rule. But the latter got the sticky end of the stick. The 6-Metres became more and more expensive to build and after the war the International Rule virtually disappeared. So after ten years the same problem of which class was to battle for the Cup cropped up again. This faced both the guardians of the Cup and those who were bent on recovering it. The J Class was quite out of the question. They were ruinously expensive before the war; now they were unthinkable. However, if the British were determined not to abandon their quest for the Cup, the Americans for their part, represented by the New York Yacht Club, were equally firm in their intent that the trophy

A Royal Visit. His Royal Highness Prince Philip, Duke of Edinburgh, is at the helm. Beside him to his right in Sovereign's cockpit is his friend and sometimes crew, sometimes skipper, Uffa Fox. To his left, in the navigator's cockpit, is Peter Scott, President of the I.Y.R.U. and Sovereign's helmsman in the unsuccessful 1964 challenge for the America's Cup.

(continued on page 136)

The Skipper is the man who runs the crew.

*Kurrewa's spinnaker blows out. Here's a problem
for the crew as well as the sail-maker—to make
sure it doesn't happen again. For the owner?
Yet another bill.*

Iyruna

The 12-Metre as she used to be—but will never be again. A racing yacht?—certainly. But one which could give shelter to her crew as she threw about tack on tack. These boats didn't shirk a long passage and had no need of an escorting motor vessel. How many of their modern, sister Twelves with their thin titanium masts could stand up and take a breeze like this on the chin?

Year of build:	*1927*
LOA:	*67 ft. 3 in.*
LWL:	*42 ft. 6 in.*
Beam:	*12 ft.*
Draft:	*8 ft. 5 in.*
Sail area:	*2,042 sq. ft.*
Tons TM:	*32*

should not gather dust and become a mere relic in the Club's Cup room. All solutions to the problems were closely studied. Even such improbable ones as turning the whole contest into an ocean racing series or, at the other extreme, one to be fought out in centreboard dinghies were considered. In the end it was decided that the spirit of the Cup could in truth only be preserved by awarding it for a match race series between the biggest racing yachts of the age.

When it came to the choice of parameters which were not too improbable it was clear that the International Rule was more viable than the Universal Rule, which was already showing signs of disintegration under the pressures of the ordinary economics of life. There was another point in its favour too. In bringing back the International Rule as opposed to sticking to the Universal, the Americans might be said to be making a concession to their European (and generally far less well-endowed) rivals. As it happened this American bounty could be described as platonic rather than compassionate, business-like rather than magnanimous. The 12-Metres already in the United States were known to be superior to those in Britain and there were more of them in commission.

Nevertheless, the British went in with their eyes open—or should have done—and this adoption breathed a new life into the graceful Twelves. On both sides of the Atlantic masts were stepped and yachts were re-rigged. New sails were provided. Designers got down to their drawing-boards. On the British side the Royal Yacht Squadron threw down the traditional gauntlet and called four eminent designers to the task of drawing out the new challenger— each to produce two designs, one in the classic form and the other a design which could be modified, improved and developed. The eight models were tank tested—and the chosen design was one of David Boyd's which came to the challenge as *Sceptre*. She was built at the yard of Alex. Robertson & Sons on the shores of Holy Loch and launched in April 1958.

The Americans were also justified in the faith they put in their system of eliminating trials. It might have been the heyday of J Class Cup racing. They built three new contenders for the defence, of which one would be chosen to face up to the British challenger. There was *Columbia* by Olin Stephens, *Easterner* by Ray Hunt and *Weatherly* by Phil Rhodes. Moreover the defence had at its disposal as a pacemaker and yardstick the Olin Stephens 12-Metre *Vim*, a boat which had swept the board in the last regattas before the war. The eliminators were won by *Columbia* who benefited in more than one way from the boats she had beaten. Taking all things into account no one gave much for the British chances. However the rout, which is all the *Sceptre–Columbia* match of September 1958 can be described as, took everyone by surprise. *Columbia* won her four races by margins varying between

7 and 12 minutes. Taking the speed of these boats into calculation this represented over a mile in distance. Various reasons have been advanced to explain the wide margin of defeat. Suffice it to say that this was the first post-war challenge and the first to be executed in 12-Metres. With *Vim* Olin Stephens had out-designed all other Twelves before the Second World War. It was hardly surprising that his superiority continued after the war was over.

After such a fiasco one would have supposed that 12-Metre racing was doomed. The post-war American Twelve was something very different from her predecessors. She was conceived for the light, early autumn breezes off Newport, Rhode Island. Dismasting or rigging failure in winds of Force 5 was accepted as a calculated risk. The British challengers had little opportunity to sharpen up in the light stuff since by and large British weather isn't built that way. Moreover the Americans had another 'secret weapon' which revealed itself only too effectively. Again it was one which the challenger was in no position to beat off. Elimination trials between several boats, each of which had high hopes (having gone to so much care, trouble and quite astronomical expense) of being chosen as the defender sometimes produced startling results. Not only did they force preconceived ideas back into the arena for a most searching scrutiny, but new ideas and innovations were constantly brought forward to the same proving ground to prove or disprove their worth. Finally, the actual elimination trials themselves, prolonged to the last minute before the moment of decision, served as a tuning up series of incomparable efficacy.

As it so often turned out, any one of a whole batch of defenders was capable of dealing summarily with the challenger. If the remedy was known to those who reached out for the Cup there was little chance of putting it into effect. In the first place, on the wrong side of the Atlantic there weren't the syndicates around to support the building of a fleet of Twelves. Furthermore no one was willing to lay out a great deal of money building a challenger without a guarantee that he would soon be off to America to try his luck.

However, contrary to the intelligent guesses of intelligent men, more than one challenge fluttered around the august eaves of the New York Yacht Club. The accepted challenge for a contest in 1964 was also a bit of a surprise. The lot fell on Australia, and although in Britain there was at first some shock at seeing what had always been regarded as a British Grail held out to another (albeit sister) country, in the world at large it was the concensus that the Australians, whose sailing has for practical purposes the status of a national sport, were as good as anybody for the job.

Came the actual struggle and, as in past history, it was a yacht eliminated from the previous defence of the Cup which won those

(*continued on page 139*)

The Twelve-Metres (continued)

COLUMBIA

*Columbia, a Sparkman and Stephens creation,
opened a new chapter in the story of the America's
Cup. She was the first winner of the trophy in the
12-Metre class, and her qualities as much as her
success helped generate a new interest in the
Twelves. In this photograph by Keith Beken it all
looks so easy!*

Year of build:	*1958*
LOA:	*69 ft. 7 in.*
LWL:	*46 ft.*
Beam:	*11 ft. 10 in.*
Draft	*9 ft.*
Sail area:	*1,950 sq. ft.*
Nett tonnage:	*25*

current at this time. *Weatherly* took the eliminators and the honour of defending the American colours. She had been much modified and she benefited by having a helmsman who, over the years, was to prove himself practically unbeatable at the helm of a 12-Metre, Emil ('Bus') Mosbacher. Mosbacher was to show, as if it were necessary, that tuning a Twelve counted for almost as much as the genius of the designer himself.

To surprised eyebrows everywhere *Gretel*, the Australian challenger, proved a redoubtable nut to crack. In certain respects she was possibly superior to *Weatherly*. Her design did not lack for originality while at the same time she borrowed from American technology the best it had to offer. Yet, paradoxically, *Gretel*'s honourable defeat by four races to one was curiously depressing. Although all experts were agreed on the magnificent way the Australian boat was sailed, it appeared little by little but finally without doubt that Mosbacher had Jock Sturrock, the brilliant Australian helmsman and an Olympic medallist in his own right, sewn up. Mosbacher, outclassed in terms of ultimate speed, had a devilish ability, which he exploited to the full, of placing himself in an attacking lee bow position. From here he squeezed his adversary quite mercilessly. When Sturrock had fallen into his wake he covered him remorselessly tack for tack.

These particular tacking duels have gone down in yachting history as classics of yacht racing.

Alan Payne, *Gretel*'s designer, had foreseen this situation. To combat it he had contrived to link the two 'coffee-grinders' together, thus significantly cutting the time needed to crank in the genoa. But Mosbacher had been watching his adversary closely. It is said that he noticed that when Sturrock was preparing to make a false tack (a manœuvre which Heckstall-Smith describes so vividly on page 80, showing how little there is that is new in racing tactics) he stood differently at the wheel. All the Australian feints were thereby signalled in advance to the American boat. On another occasion and reaching under spinnaker, *Gretel* was overhauling *Weatherly* at a significant rate. The finishing line was no great distance away and it was clear that the American lead would not hold out. The quick thinking Americans handed their spinnaker and ran up the genoa. Believing they were sailing into a heading wind-shift the Australians followed suit. The result? Both yachts proceeded at roughly equal speeds to the finish—with *Weatherly* holding her lead all the way to the line. This encounter showed that even with a better boat the challengers couldn't necessarily win, while the defenders for their part realized the danger inherent in having to rely on the superior quality of their helmsmen.

Those in charge at the New York Yacht Club made it known that henceforward challengers would have to be entirely designed, built and equipped in their own countries. This meant

(continued on page 142)

	EVAINE 
Year of build:	1936
LOA:	69 ft. 11 in.
LWL:	45 ft. 8 in.
Beam:	11 ft. 10 in.
Draft:	8 ft. 11 in.
Sail area:	1,900 sq. ft.
Tons TM:	34

	SCEPTRE ▼
Year of build:	1958
LOA:	68 ft. 11 in.
LWL:	46 ft. 6 in.
Beam:	11 ft. 10 in.
Draft:	9 ft.
Sail area:	1,900 sq. ft.
Tons TM:	35

Sceptre and Evaine

To serve as a trial horse for *Sceptre,* Britain's first challenger for the America's Cup after the Second World War, the old pre-war Twelve *Evaine,* designed by Charles E. Nicholson and built by Camper & Nicholson in 1936, was re-fitted and modernized as far as was possible. Her sails and gear were just as good as *Sceptre*'s, although in the photograph of the cockpit arrangements above, we can see the trend towards separate cockpits for the navigator as well as the helmsman, which isolated them from the hurly-burly of the crew's work and facilitated the mounting of an efficient mainsheet horse.

In a choppy Solent with a good breeze, *Evaine*

tries to sit on *Sceptre.* Neither boat is able to carry a big genoa and *Sceptre* appears to be slightly the stiffer of the two. An unusual sight on a 12-Metre nowadays — and on many other boats and dinghies for that matter — would be a burgee flying at the masthead. This is where wind direction and speed indicators are now fitted as science comes more and more to the aid of instinct in yacht racing.

At the time of writing (April 1969) *Sceptre* is owned by Erik Maxwell, who may yet himself shoulder the burden of another British challenge for the America's Cup.

The Twelve-Metres (continued)

CONSTELLATION
Year of build: 1964
LOA: 68 ft. 5 in.
LWL: 46 ft.
Beam: 11 ft. 11 in.
Draft: 8 ft. 11 in.
Sail area: Not revealed
Tons TM: 35

Constellation alone and miles in the lead. She was faster, closer winded, better in a chop and crewed to perfection. Although her challenger Sovereign had on the whole the better of the starts, the British boat never really gave the defender a moment's uneasiness once the line was crossed.

that American sails and even American sailcloth were barred to challengers and that access to the Stevens tank was denied to foreign designers. In spite of this a new challenge was forthcoming for a confrontation at the earliest possible date even if this meant waiting three years, the minimum interval that the Committee of the New York Yacht Club was now prepared to entertain. The British challengers, the Royal Thames Yacht Club and Anthony Boyden, went once more to David Boyd and the yard of Alex. Robertson & Sons. There was sense in this since lessons had been learned from the *Sceptre* fiasco and the Australians in *Gretel* had shown that the Americans could be rattled and beaten. The new British boat, *Sovereign*, was very beautiful indeed. David Boyd is incapable of drawing an ugly boat, but in this challenger he produced a work of art, and she was a good performer too.

Unexpected help for the 'Old Country's' challenger came from two remarkable Australian brothers, Frank and John Livingston. They went to David Boyd and Alex. Robertson & Sons and built what was as near as one could get to a sistership to *Sovereign*. Again the thinking was acceptable. Two identical boats would mean the closest possible racing for selection and a premium on the best helmsman and crew. The Livingstons built *Kurrewa V*, but it was yachtsman Owen Aisher who commissioned her, fitted her out and campaigned her. If the

British were still groping in the dark when it came to design development, they were at least now able to get closer to the Americans in the matters of tuning and crew training.

Everything about this 1964 challenge proved misleading. Yachting journalists following every detail of building and training gave the challengers an entirely false idea of their competence. The choice of those to run the show was not only based on technical criteria but also on social ones. There was no lack of differences, even quarrels betweens persons of influence, and the wider vision and single-mindedness of purpose without which one can do nothing valuable was never achieved. The eliminators were simplified by the defection of *Kurrewa*, aboard which it seemed impossible to strike an understanding between the helmsmen and the crew. Sailmakers and manufacturers of sailcloth, in spite of all efforts to catch up on American technology in this sector, failed to bring home the bacon.

On the other side of the Atlantic the Americans had moved on. They had been far from happy about the *Weatherly* defence against *Gretel* and recognized that they had stood in greater danger of losing the Cup than at any time since *Endeavour*'s challenge in 1934. So the 1964 challenge became the occasion for pulling out all the stops. In the lovely *Constellation* they simply had a boat that was better than a good British boat—and they also had a very cool customer in command, Bob Bavier. The result of all this was another and

greater fiasco, as *Sovereign* went down 4–0. The difference between the two boats' performances created a record of a kind for the history of the Cup. We are speaking of intervals at the finish of the order of twenty minutes and with the slight haze the boats weren't even in sight of each other when *Constellation* took her gun.

Elsewhere things started to move rapidly. The very first race showed how the series would end up and Sir Frank Packer, head of the syndicate which had built *Gretel*, sent an envelope to the chairman of the Cup Committee of the New York Yacht Club. The chairman went through the motions and refused to open it until after the last race. It was only too obvious that a new challenge was on its way, but the Cup Committee observed a rule that a new challenge could not be discussed while an existing one was still in progress.

The Australians went to work. They went after American techniques, elimination trials and sailcloth research. Predictably, a few months before the new encounter it was announced that a breakthrough had been achieved and that the challenger would have sailcloth that was streets ahead of the American tissue. However, when it came to the tuning-up a less optimistic note was to be heard. There were frequent changes of helmsmen and the sounds of argument were everywhere abroad. There were also technical troubles and dismastings in particular occurred with disquieting frequency.

The new challenger *Dame Pattie* (another touch of the cap brim) eliminated *Gretel*. The latter, however, had been much altered and no one could really rate performance with exactitude. While all this was going on the Americans placed an order for only one boat. When it was learned that 'the syndicate' had obtained the services of Olin Stephens (designer of *Vim*, *Columbia* and *Constellation*) and Bus Mosbacher, no one else felt like chancing his arm, and in the end there was only a tentative shy from California with a much modified *Columbia*.

The *Intrepid* v. *Dame Pattie* contest in September 1967 (*Intrepid*, traditionally, took her name from a famous ship of the American Navy) was an almost boring repeat performance of what had gone before. From the first race the Australians realized the fate in store for them. In the subsequent races they did their jobs impeccably but without much conviction.

Now there was to be a new turn of events. Marcel Bich, a French industrialist, entered the arena. In succession *Constellation*, *Sovereign* and *Kurrewa* passed into the hands of the French Committee for the America's Cup. Naval architect André Mauric was charged with designing a challenger. That the debut of these yachts as French 12-Metres was attended by wailing and gnashing of Gallic teeth goes without saying. In spite of this it became clearer and clearer as time went by that Marcel Bich had done his homework and had no intention of making the same mistakes as the other challengers. His objective seemed to be to get to grips as quickly as possible with the problems inevitably conjoined to an enterprize of this scale and to attack the Americans with the minimum of delay.

The first part of his plan went as he wished. Regular racing at Hyères gradually sorted out helmsmen, crew and after-guards. The last part of his schedule did not run so smoothly. 12-Metre fever was raging on a continental scale. A syndicate of Greek shipowners wanted to place King Constantine, Dragon Olympic gold medallist, at the helm of a Greek Twelve; the British and Australians were arguing with France about the next challenge; in America itself there was talk of two Californian syndicates and one from Detroit. The problem was resolved when the New York Yacht Club accepted the Australian gauntlet on condition that the Aussies agreed to international eliminators between their challenger and any of the other pretenders who presented themselves off Newport before the Cup series — the winner of such pre-race eliminators to be the boat to challenge for the Cup. Nobody knows what the future has in store nor how all these people who have devoted their resources, their time, their skill and their money to a fight for a silver jug will be paid for their pains. It's certain, however, that henceforth the Twelves will take a new lease of life and that in the near future many countries will have one or more of these magnificent yachts!

The 12-Metres have their faults: notably the impossibility of transforming them economically to offshore racing or cruising. They also have two great virtues. The hull lasts a long time. If one has a good boat she can be raced for many a year and even if her chances of winning are diminished, her capability as a trainer of helmsmen and crews is not one whit lessened. The second advantage is that she needs a crew of eleven or twelve. In a period of intensive training it is normal to have two crews per boat and because nobody can be at it all the year round there are hundreds of berths to be filled. Whether the Cup is won or lost this competition gives rise to a new form of nautical athleticism and is providing a significant number of young men with an experience of top class competition which they will remember for a long time. Relieving the New York Yacht Club of the responsibility for cleaning 'that old mug', a responsibility they have held since 1851, would be a wonderful spur to international yacht racing — and justify the devotion of those three gallant gentlemen, the Earl of Dunraven, Sir Thomas Lipton and Sir Thomas Sopwith, not to mention those gallant souls who crewed the British challengers over the years. By repute, should the glass case on 44th Street have to give up the Cup, its place will be taken by the head of the losing American helmsman. One hates to see the end of a good sailor — but the odds are getting better.

Flica II

Flinging themselves into the preparation of new 12-Metres the new generation of crews showed more enthusiasm than experience. This rather show-off photograph at least serves to prove that the will was there to adopt every means towards making the boat go faster, even if the result was rather to freeze the crew than improve *Flica's* performance.

Flica II was designed by Laurent Giles and built by Fife's at Fairlie in 1939. She always seems to pile up a heavy quarter wave, as can be seen in this photograph.

Year of build:	*1939*
LOA:	*67 ft. 1 in.*
LWL:	*46 ft. 6 in.*
Beam:	*11 ft. 9 in.*
Draft:	*9 ft.*
Sail area:	—
Tons TM:	*34*

International One Design ▶
LOA:	33 ft. 4 in.
LWL:	21 ft. 6 in.
Beam:	6 ft. 9 in.
Draft:	5 ft. 4 in.
Sail area:	418 sq. ft.
Displacement:	6,950 lb.

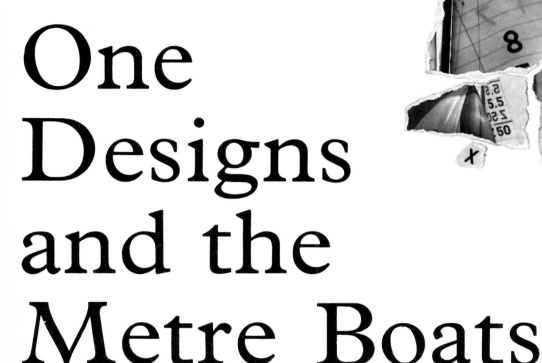

One Designs and the Metre Boats

As predictable as the decline of the Big Boats and the Restricted Classes was the rise of the One Designs. It was practically impossible to build identical boats at the 60 feet Length Over All level or, once built, to keep them identical over the years. On the contrary it was important to allow an owner in the course of the long career that his yacht was capable of providing, the opportunity of modernizing her and of bringing her up-to-date with the latest ideas and practices. Nevertheless for a large number of racing yachtsmen it was equally important that their craft should realize a reasonable 'secondhand' value and that winning guns should be the fruit of the superior skills of helmsmen and crews rather than the innate superiority of the design of the boat itself.

From this stemmed the popularity of the One Designs and, as sailing came more and more within the reach of the general public, the Class dinghies which are now numbered in fleets. One of the most popular One Designs is the IOD, the International One Design, which can be seen in all the tension of a race in the photograph on the following two pages of *Wahoo*, as she dices with the East Gurnard buoy off Cowes.

The IODs are to the design of Bjarne Aas. Moreoever the IOD has had to be built by Aas. This is the logic of one-designmanship. Apart from the rules themselves, building outlets must surely be limited to one yard—one favourite son. More than one builder?—and one will always try and steal a march over another. With one outlet only it will be in the builder's best interests to make all the boats exactly the same. He can buy materials and equipment in bulk and his men can build the boats in their sleep.

It was the Clyde Club, the Royal Northern, which introduced the Dragon from Norway. It was the Royal Corinthian at Burnham-on-Crouch in Essex which brought us face to face with the IOD.

A Race in a 6-Metre—1932

◀ *The photograph on pages 156–7 shows 6-Metre racing at its best—and, incidentally, demonstrates once again the Beken ability to capture the dramatic moment. Here in 1949 the trophy at stake is the British–American Cup, and battling for it in a brisk nor'-nor'-westerly as they run eastwards down the Solent towards the forts are Colonel Jack Harrison's Boyd-designed Marletta (K70), giving nothing away by running under her genoa to her spinnaker-carrying team-mate, Jimmy Hume's McGruer-designed and McGruer-built Johan (K65). But the American Llanoria (US83) is the boat to look at. An Olympic Gold Medallist, she was the last and the greatest of the 6-Metres to be built—not surprising when you see that she came from the Sparkman and Stephens design office. Within minutes of this photograph being taken she broke through the lee of the British pair to take the lead and hold it to the line.*

(PAGES 156–157)

To BE asked aboard *Vorsa* as local pilot, for the races off Cowes against the Americans, was very flattering. As our Committee did not (in view of the straightforward tides there) think I would be very valuable for the races off Ryde, I was able to race my canoe at Langston during those three days.

Each night I rang up home in order to hear how the British team had fared, and the news was not good, the American team being first, second, third and fourth in two races, and first, second and third in the other race. So the Americans only needed to win the first race of the Cowes series to take home the trophy.

On Thursday night, after winning the Royal Canoe Club's Challenge Cup, and attending their annual Lobster Supper at Langston, my wife and I set sail in our schooner for Cowes with *Wanderer* in the davits, arriving in the early morning light. Later that morning I met Maurice Clark and Alfred Mylne, owner and designer of *Vorsa*, on the parade, in front of the Royal London, as arranged.

We were soon aboard and sailing to the starting line off the Squadron under mainsail only. *Vorsa* had but two headsails, the working and genoa, without the intermediate, which I knew, from sailing with them, the American 'Sixes' carried and valued highly. The sky was heavy with clouds, each rain squall making up from the south-west affecting the wind in a slightly differ-ent manner as it passed. The tide was not yet high, but the narrow eddy between the Squadron and Egypt Point was running fairly strong to the westward. Such a valuable ally could not be ignored, yet to accept the help it offered meant sailing along under the lee of the land in a light fluky wind where a genoa was needed.

In order to conceal our intentions we jilled along without headsail until the last, when setting our genoa, we made for the line a fraction too soon and were recalled, being forced by competitors close aboard to sail on some distance before turning back.

So we started late, but were soon in first place, for knowing that eddy, and the strange winds encountered in it, we never once fought the foul tide running strongly 50 yards out. When the wind headed us along that shore we let *Vorsa* drive with everything shaking until the next free puff came, while the rest of the fleet bore away as the wind headed them, and were at once in the foul tide.

While we know it is wind that drives a sailing vessel, we must also remember that the tide, like the poor, we have always with us (if not against us), and where the dividing line between a foul tide and a fair eddy is so sharply defined the tides are all important. That foul tide was running at 3 knots and the fair eddy at 1 knot, and as a 6-metre's speed dead to windward is $3\frac{1}{2}$ knots it is only possible for her to make good $\frac{1}{2}$ knot to windward against a foul tide of 3 knots, but by creeping along the shore (as *Vorsa* did) at an average of 4 knots in the fair eddy the speed over the ground becomes 5 knots.

This easily explains how *Vorsa* came from last into first place in the short beat from the Squadron to Egypt Point, where we stood across at once for the easier tide under the north shore. Once to the north of Lepe we were in less tide,

Back to the IODs again in the photograph on the next two pages. The experts would say that in this squall it would be wise to ease the mainsheet to take the load off Flirt and to keep that tumbling wave to leeward out of the cockpit. But that is an easy thing for the expert to say from his fireside, and what an instant reaction of energy and decision is demanded of the helmsman when a puff like this hits the boat. Incidentally, the helmsman in this instance is a helmswoman—Clare Connell, daughter of the famous yachtsman Owen Aisher and sister of Robin Aisher, the 5·5-Metre Bronze Medallist in the 1968 Olympic Games.
(PAGES 160–161)

and thinking *Vorsa* would do even better with her working instead of her genoa headsail we changed, and this was our undoing, for two American 'Sixes' caught and passed us in the beat along the north shore, so we rounded West Lepe third, but by taking a great circle course to the south into stronger tide we picked up one place on the run to West Bramble and held our second place round Old Castle Point buoy, through the line to Egypt Point. Then the intermediate jibs of the Americans told their tale again, and two of them passed us in the hard going to windward to East Lepe, so that we rounded there fourth, but hard upon their heels.

We again took our great circle course southward into the last of the main flood, whilst the Americans sailed the straight course to West Bramble, in, if any, a foul tide. We arrived at West Bramble first, but only by inches.

Olin badly wanted to put *Nancy* in between us and the buoy, but Alfred Mylne watched him like a cat with a mouse, and as he darted for our weather Alfred said, 'No, no, laddie', as firmly as a policeman on point duty.

Rebuking Olin as he did, Alfred Mylne looked every inch a policeman, even to the brawny 'police muscles.'[1] And so we rounded first, but as soon as the protection to weather the buoy had given us was left astern, the four American boats were upon us like a pack of hungry wolves, two to weather, one astern, and one to leeward. Our best course to the next mark was a great circle course to leeward, for here the very last of the flood was still with us, while in Cowes Roads it had turned against us.

But a 'Six' reaching is faster than one running,

and the two reaching to windward would soon take our wind and then run past us unless we defended our weather by luffing towards Cowes and the foul tide.

Oh for an equal fight! For some of our team alongside to help, or to go through into the lead to leeward while we took three Americans the longest way home. And so we luffed and luffed into Cowes Roads, while *Bob Kat*, the last American boat round the West Bramble buoy, carried on her own sweet way to leeward, and arrived at Old Castle Point buoy with a minute lead, next came *Jill*, then we in *Vorsa*.

Once round the buoy the fair tide through the Roads made the close reach home very short and we finished as we rounded, *Vorsa* coming in behind two and in front of two of the invincible American team.

It was a relief to allow our tense nerves to slacken back to normal again, and give three cheers for such victors.

	H.	M.	S.
Bob Kat (American),			
Robert B. Meyer	3	5	51
Jill (American), J. Seward Johnson	3	6	54
Vorsa (British), Maurice Clark ..	3	7	9
Nancy (American), Olin Stephens	3	7	11
Lucie (American),			
Briggs S. Cunningham	3	7	24
Nada (British), F. G. Mitchell ..	3	7	50
Ancora II (British), Cyril Wright	3	8	36
Finetta (British), James S. Bacon	3	15	26

Points: America, 24½; Britain, 12.

Uffa Fox: *Sailing, Seamanship and Yacht Construction.* 1934

'Police muscles': The full midship section usually found under a policeman's waistcoat.

In the Wake of the Giants

The photograph on the preceeding pages illustrates one of the classic contests of the era, the fight in the 6-Metre class between American and British teams for the British–American Cup. This was 1949. The windward yacht is Britain's Lalage. She is fighting it out with the famous American, Goose, which is attacking from leeward. Lalage is hard on the wind and pointing high. At this moment the American eased sheets fractionally and bore away by a couple of inches. She sailed through Lalage's lee so closely that her quarter wave came aboard the British boat and nearly filled her cockpit! The British–American Cup was one of the most exciting series in the 6-Metre class and provided splendid sport.

◄ *LALAGE*
Year of build: 1936
LOA: 37·4 ft.
LWL: 23·3 ft.
Beam: 6·5 ft.
Draft   5·4 ft.
Sail area: 450 sq. ft.
Tons TM: 5

◄ *GOOSE*
Year of build: 1938
LOA: 37·0 ft.
LWL: 23·7 ft.
Beam: 6·0 ft.
Draft: 5·4 ft.
Sail area: Not revealed
Tons TM: 5

FIRECRACKER ►
Year of build: 1936
LOA: 35·7 ft.
LWL: 23·5 ft.
Beam: 6·17 ft.
Draft: 5·4 ft.
Sail area: 467 sq. ft.
Tons TM: 5

In the 1951 British–American Cup series there was an American boat called Firecracker. She was an old boat, face-lifted, brought right up to date and carving her last niche in yachting history. Her helmsman cuts out a silhouette which has since become familiar. He is Bus Mosbacher, who was to develop into the most famous and skilful of all helmsmen in the Twelves and the 'big time' of the America's Cup.

THE 6-Metre Class International Rule first appeared on the scene in 1921. However the in-fighting had started some time before that on the drawing-boards of designers and in the yards of the United States, Great Britain, Scandinavia and the rest of Europe. Adopted for the Olympic Games right up to 1952 the Sixes provided the most 'needle' and costly racing in the game. Fine helmsman, dedicated crews and the best that sailmakers, spar makers and experts in rigging and fittings could provide—those were the ingredients that the Sixes provided when they met in combat. The Grands Prix of the 6-Metre class were the British–American Cup, the Seawanhaka Cup, the Scandinavian Gold Cup and the French One Ton Cup. If American supremacy was undeniable in the J Class things were much more open in the Sixes. The Scandinavians did better than most and particularly with *Maybe VI*. It was they who at the Genoa regattas had invented and put into practice the genoa jib with its tremendous overlap. European yacht yards stretched themselves to build these beautiful boats where weight-saving above the water line and aloft was the constant aim. The famous *Ylliam IX* was Swiss-built to designs of Olin Stephens. A whole family of Sixes was designed and built in Scotland at the hands of McGruer and David Boyd—and Boyd went on later to design both *Sceptre* and *Sovereign*. Among other famous names to come from Scotland was *Elghi III* in which Meunier du Houssoye captured the One Ton Cup before the Cercle de la Voile de Paris re-allocated it to another race series.

But notwithstanding all their manifest qualities, the Sixes were expensive boats. Moreover as an owner one was always having to up sticks and high-tail it to the U.S.A. or to Genoa, or to Scandinavia or to the Solent. But this of course was the penalty and the privilege of owning a real racing yacht and of being admitted to a most exclusive club whose members chose to meet up practically anywhere in the world. If one was beaten, say, at Kiel, one could always take one's revenge at Cannes or Torquay. . . .

The Skerry Cruisers

This 30 Square Metre is the first in a line of Sunmaids owned by Guy Bowles. The present Sunmaid is a British One Ton Cup boat.

THE SKERRY Cruiser or Square Metre Rule was an experiment which ought to have been pursued further and should have been developed over a very much longer period of time. It started with a Sail Area Rule which first made its appearance in 1920 in the Baltic. The only factor was the amount of sail carried and boats built to the rule raced without handicap in the following categories: 15 square metres, 22, 30, 45, 100, 150 and 250 square metres. The parameters of the hull had to comply with certain limitations but these had no effect on the sail area measurement. Rigging and sail plans therefore came out of the latest in aero-dynamic practice which dictated a very high aspect ratio rig. There was a certain tolerance in the measurements of the jib which led to an astounding amount of overlap and the 'liberality' — one will not say looseness — of the controls on the hull led to surprisingly happy results. These long, very light yachts proved themselves extremely fast and remarkably seaworthy. There were those who hoped that the 30 Square Metres for instance — of which *Sunmaid* is shown on the facing page — would displace the Sixes, which cost nearly double the money.

The Skerry Cruisers found some enthusiastic partisans over in England. Uffa Fox caught the bug and himself designed and built *Avocet* and *Waterwitch*. Francis Herreshoff succumbed to the same infection and imported *Glauckoff* into the U.S.A., promptly renaming her *Visitor*.

The man who was to invent the Single-Handed Transatlantic Race and the Round Britain Race, H. G. 'Blondie' Hasler, took the R.O.R.C. championship with the 30 Square Metre *Tre-Sang*. These wonderful boats, as long so to speak as the Viking longships, would beat the Sixes in a breeze but were outdistanced by their more firmly established rivals in the light stuff.

Doubtless the 'Square Metres' lacked a strong international organization. The Rule was interpreted in many different ways in many different countries. Local mutations appeared and the letter of the rule came to be observed to the detriment of the spirit. Thus it came about that in the United States the boats were built to a translation of the German translation of the rule. Even in Sweden there appeared widely differing versions of the same rule category. Generally speaking a way was found of getting round the sail area limitations — which were after all the focal point and the spirit of the rule — and boats built with this advantage effectively killed off all competition. Thus it was that the Skerry Cruisers, while esteemed by all and sundry, gradually sailed into limbo — except perhaps for South African waters where a handful are still racing and giving their owners tremendous pleasure.

Dragon Race—1958

THE RACE is from the Royal Yacht Squadron line at Cowes, to my mind the finest starting line in the world, for there is the committee ashore firm and steadfast as the platform on which they stand, for they are standing on the battlements and looking through the gun-ports of Henry VIII's castle. Here they have a clear view all over the course with their powerful glasses, and are in reach of the telephone in case of an accident. They can summon a doctor, a lifeboat, or a tug, as required and can stay there comfortably all day and night as they have food and drink at hand. In front of them are the twenty-two lovely gun-metal cannons presented to the Club by King Edward VII and so they have plenty of recall guns and reserves, and the flagpole from which the signals are flying was the mast of the Marquis of Ailsa's famous old racing cutter the *Bloodhound*. The line is long, perhaps too long, because there is so much room on it for the starters that it is often extremely difficult to judge the best place on it for the start. For though, with the south-west wind, the inner end is to windward, here you have less wind and also less tide. Although I have lived at Cowes and raced its waters some fifty years, I had never judged a start so well as the other boats I'd been racing against in the previous four races. This is the final race for Prince Philip's Cup, given for competition between the four Cowes Clubs, The Royal Yacht Squadron, The Royal Corinthian Yacht Club, The Royal London Yacht Club, The Island Sailing Club, also The Imperial Poona Yacht Club. In this series of races, there is also a prize for the best boat. It is an extremely interesting series of races because the helmsmen and crew change boats every race, so that at the end of the series each club has raced every boat and there is a champion club, as well as a champion boat....

Kenneth Preston, sailing for the Island Sailing Club is well ahead on points, with Pat Dyas, Commodore of, and sailing for, the Royal Corinthian Yacht Club, second. So as we manœuvre on the starting line I am trying to balance up the best point at which to cross the line when the starting gun goes.

BOOM! Off goes the ten minute cannon, as Class flag D for Dragon breaks out from the yardarm. The International Code Flag O has been hoisted at the west yardarm for half an hour to indicate that we are going to the westward leaving all marks to starboard. There is no worry as to the course, for the letter C was hung over the battlements telling us that we were going to round a mark off Gurnard, then round the North East Gurnard in Stansore Bay, round the East Bramble to the line. Once round the distance is nine miles. A wonderful course, as it gave us two plugs to windward, a reach and a dead run, so testing helmsmen, crew, boats, sails and gear on all points of sailing.

This time, I decided I would start to leeward of the fleet where I would have more wind and more tide. Although I would be under the lee of the other four boats when starting, this was partly compensated for by the increased wind and tide, and also that when I came in upon them I should be on the starboard tack with right of way while they, on the port, would have to keep clear.

The boat I was most worried about in this race was *Bluebottle*, jointly owned by Her Majesty the Queen and Prince Philip, Duke of Edinburgh, for she's always loved a breeze and has been good at stamping her way to windward in a jump of a sea.

BOOM! The five minute and the Blue Peter cannon, and now we are under starter's orders when all the racing rules apply, and we can be disqualified for infringing any of these from this moment on till we finally cross the finishing line. During this time the boats have no proper course and all five are twisting and turning, tacking and gybing, for all the world like swallows darting about the skies in search of food, and missing each other by inches without colliding.

I came inshore on the starboard tack which

has the right of way, and then, a minute to the starting gun, tacked over to port, started reaching down the line almost dead to leeward on the port tack, on which course I had to keep out of the way of every other boat racing. Such a course meant that when the starting gun went I should be travelling fast through being so far off the wind, and being close on the line would only have to sharpen up and lay my boat hard on the wind for the drive to windward down into Gurnard Bay. This, as well as giving us a start with a lot of way on, also meant that there could be no hitch in setting up the jib or the runner, we had only to sail away on our course, free from interference from any of the other boats.

BOOM! The starting cannon! Down comes the class flag and Blue Peter and away we go, slowly but surely and relentlessly. The *Pioneer* which I was sailing started to forge ahead and also come up higher on the wind than the other four Dragons, and after a while we had them all well back though up on our weather quarter, for meantime, they were tacking to and fro to clear the wind from each other. Then, not wishing to get too far away from the rest of them, we tacked to port and stood in to see just how we were doing with them. Sure enough *Bluebottle* was the leader of this fleet and as we came in we crossed her on the starboard tack, and then threw about on her weather, but we were slow getting in our jib sheets and she escaped through our lee with a clear wind, and now we held her where she was for she was so close to leeward that she could not tack for the Gurnard Mark until we did. Once we tacked we were dead ahead of her by a couple of boat's lengths, and rounded this mark in a flurry of foam, the first boat of the fleet, with all the others coming along close on our heels.

It was all very exciting sailing, the flying spray going half-way up the mainsail and the headsail, and the boat plunging deeply into every fifth or seventh wave and shooting green water right over the cabin top and into the cockpit.

Now we eased our sheets, both headsail and main, and started a wild scamper across to the north shore to round our next mark in Stansore Bay.

Normally, with the wind and tide in this direction we should all have carried spinnakers, but a spinnaker with this weight of wind so far on the beam would have hove a Dragon down on her beam ends and filled her up. So none of us set spinnakers on this reach, because our terrific speed brought the wind a point forward of the beam. All the way across, *Bluebottle* (second) was continually luffing out to weather to try and take our wind in spite of the fact that all of us had more wind then we really needed. This we could not allow, for although being down to leeward would mean we had the turn at the mark, there was always the possibility of a Dragon scooting out straight ahead. So as *Bluebottle* luffed, we luffed, and kept the weather gauge,

until finally she was content to try and get an overlap to leeward, and so have the turn at the mark, and as we did not think she could do this we were also content.

Meantime the Royal Yacht Squadron's boat, being sailed by John Raymond, had carried away a lower shroud and had to retire, so there were four of us left in the race. Three parts of the way across the Island Sailing Club boat started luffing out across our stern, and luffing with him was the Royal Corinthian Yacht Club boat. As these two were first and second for the Cup with only two points between them, I decided not to go luffing out with them, but to let them have their own battle in peace in case any of my actions favoured one or the other of these two, one of which was bound to win the trophy. So *Blue-bottle* and *Pioneer* kept away for the mark and left these two to fight their own battle out unmolested.

Bluebottle was still trying to establish an overlap to leeward, and so have the turn of the mark and have the joy of rounding first.

All was well. We arrived at the mark first with a boat's length of clear water between us and the second boat, and we gybed round fairly comfortably in spite of all the wind and sea. I did so at the moment we were in the lee of *Bluebottle* and the buoy and away we chased for the East Bramble buoy some three miles off.

Bluebottle swiftly gybed round the buoy and rushed off out to windward, but this I did not mind as she was going into more tide which was now against us.

At the end of Cowes Week, we are at the end of the normal sailing season for now is the time when all should be up in Scotland shooting the wily grouse, and so the gear on all the boats is suffering from a season of hard sailing. In the previous race the Royal Yacht Squadron crew had carried away the spinnaker halyard on *Pioneer*, so we had no spinnaker halyard and this meant that we had to lower and stow our headsail, shackle the spinnaker on to this halyard and then hoist it. What with the jumping about in the seaway with a wet and slippery deck underneath him, John Chamier let the shackle pin overboard as he went to put this into the head of the spinnaker. So Reggie Bennett, the other member of the crew, and I started looking through the various drawers on *Pioneer* for another shackle found one and also the shackle opener and passed them forward to John, who shackled the jib halyard to the head of the spinnaker....

The other three boats having no spinnaker trouble hoisted their spinnakers and now were all ahead of us. Once our spinnaker was up we started to quietly overhaul the others who were farther out and to the south against the stronger tide than we were as we scooted over the Bramble Bank.

I knew full well that Kenneth Preston, sailing for the Island Sailing Club, would be anxious about his own boat which we were sailing, going over the Bramble Bank. For a great many years during the equinox of September, I've held cricket matches on the Brambles, so had no intention of spoiling our cricket pitch by ploughing a deep rut in it with our keel, and so slowly but surely, we started to win back the ground lost to the others through having no spinnaker halyard, on this wild and exciting run.

We had trimmed our mainsail, with a main boom as far out as it would go without letting the top of the sail beyond the cross-tree and forward of the mast. This gives a boat a weather roll and once you start this rolling, life on board is wearisome and terrifying. We had also set our spinnaker so that its weather luff was continually on edge, and this meant that the boom was as far aft as it could possibly be. The sheet was also out—perhaps a little farther than it should be—so that everything that went into the spinnaker was pushing the boat right ahead and not pressing her. I, for my part, had to steer the boat without letting the spinnaker collapse, keeping as far to leeward of the rest of the fleet as possible to ease the tide and keep our wind free. Sailing this way, we went right through the fleet out into first place, but at the end of the run we had to lower our spinnaker long before we need have done so for the changing over of the halyard, just in case we had another mishap with the shackle. This let *Bluebottle* around the buoy a boat's length ahead of us in second place, with the Corinthian boat third and the Island Sailing Club boat fourth.

When you round a buoy running against the tide, the first boat round has the advantage of the tide taking her to windward of the mark before the other boat rounds, so it is generally fair and square right upon the wind of the next boat behind. Knowing that, I went away in a wide sweep so that we could luff smartly round the buoy and get ourselves if possible even to windward of the position of the boat ahead which has been taken to windward by the tide. This we managed to do, and so we came round astern, with a loss of way to the Royal London Club boat *Bluebottle*, but with our wind clear.

Directly we had our sheets trimmed home I tucked the crew in the cabin up to windward where the windage was nil, and where their weight would do most good, and there they could rest quietly and calmly away from the blustering wind and spray. So we started our exciting, heavy, and arduous drive to windward towards the Royal Yacht Squadron's finishing line.

I've always been at my best in blowing weather. Off the wind we'd driven our little Dragon so hard that at times she had her stemhead some two feet under the wave ahead with water running over the cabin top and into the cockpit, and water running over the afterdeck, all at the same time, and had so bludgeoned her through into the lead. Once she'd come out of this she'd be on the top of a wave and would go surfing down the face of it in a wild exhilarating ride. Through all this she had to be held firmly and

steadily on her course, otherwise she would broach to, take the wind abeam, be hove down on her side, and perhaps fill up.

Now we were on the wind I felt even more joyful than ever, and we quietly sailed out to weather, while still going the same speed as *Bluebottle*, a champion in this sort of going. We stood across for the Island shore and when halfway across the Solent we walked into a shift of wind which gave *Bluebottle* all the ground back which we had gained. The Glanville twins seized the opportunity and tacked immediately, and had it not been for the fact that they were on the port side they would have crossed ahead of us. But because port tack gives way to starboard they went under our stern. We tacked on top of them hoping to take their wind, but the stitching up at the cross-tree had gone in our jib, through a hard summer sailing, and as we tacked this seam caught on the end of the cross-tree and there we were hove to almost at a stand-still. This let *Bluebottle* slip quietly through our lee and away. John rushed forward, freed the jib, and we sheeted it home and away we went once more dead in the wake of *Bluebottle*, now some three lengths ahead, in exactly the same position that we had been round the buoy. Life is just one disappointment after another!

You must never miss an opportunity of complaining at your crew, when they have done something wrong, or of praising them when they have done something right, because then they know exactly where they stand, and what they are doing. So I said, 'You chaps have lost us the ground we made and so has this wind shift, but don't worry, our boat will fight it all back and be the first over the line'.

So, away we started with the race commencing all over again so far as *Bluebottle* and *Pioneer* were concerned. Slowly but surely, we worked out to windward while still going the same speed and by the time we'd arrived at the South Bramble buoy, *Pioneer* had worked a quarter mile dead to windward of *Bluebottle*, who at this point tacked to go under our stern. We made a tack for the island shore, well to windward of her, so that we did not take her wind, to make it sure that she did not get a shift of wind as before. Then when we could make the line comfortably, we tacked and crossed the line a comfortable winner of the last race, the Royal London with *Bluebottle* second, the Royal Corinthian in *Buccaneer*, third, and the Island Sailing Club in *Viking* fourth. The Island Sailing Club was still the winner of the Prince Philip Cup by two points.... The Royal Yacht Squadron, because they were the last, would again be organizing and running the race next year, choosing the course, and the boats in which we would sail. The arrangements could not be in better hands, neither could we be given better courses anywhere in the world.

Uffa Fox: *Sailing Boats.* 1959

X One Design

THE STORY of the X One Designs contains success, a remarkable mistake, and a strange stalemate. The success part of the tale is that of a one-design controlled by very strict rules and the requirement for a stout-hearted performance boat with a long life expectation. The Xs have given their owners tremendous fun without being too fast, too hair-raising, or too complex. They were born on the Isle of Wight in 1909, on the drawing-board of A. Westmacott, who designed a number of wonderful day racing boats for Solent waters, boats like the Seaview Mermaids, the Solent Sunbeams, the Yarmouth One Designs, the Royal London Y.C. One Designs, and the Bembridge One Designs. The design survived the First World War and was adopted by the Royal Motor Yacht Club at Poole. In 1928 the Bermudian rig was adopted, and at the same time a spinnaker was tried. This sail was turned down as not being suitable for the configuration of the hull! That was the mistake that passed into history and was not rectified until much later.

In 1967, 141 boats of the X Class took part in Cowes Week, which is nearly the total number built over the years! In the photograph one can see that number 14—she must date from 1920—fights the good fight against 150, one of the latest to be built.

The stalemate situation is that the Class is for practical purposes confined to the Solent and Poole Harbour and has never spread to foreign waters. Such a 'sympathetic' class deserves a wider fame.

X One Design. LOA: 20 ft. 8 in. LWL: 17 ft. 8 in. Beam: 6 ft. 6 in. Draft: 2 ft. 9 in. Sail area: 210 sq. ft.

The Star Class

IN 1909 a one-design class 17 feet overall and hard chined at that with a fin and bulb keel made a hit on Manhasset Bay, Long Island. Several owners with 'Buggs' Hanneton's (that was his name) boats thought that a similar design but a little bigger could become a splendid and exciting monotype at a reasonable cost. At their request the naval architect William Garden in 1911 designed the Star, and the builder Ike Smith of Port Washington, Long Island, built the first twenty-two boats for $260 apiece. That was the 'economic boat' which under the avuncular eyes of her promoters George Corry and George Elder was in forty years to spread all over the world, attract the élite of helmsmen and—one has to admit it—become the archetype of the sophisticated and costly race boat. But the heyday of the Star was to turn on itself. The fact that the boat was a one-design had been the seed of its remarkable growth. Perhaps this has become an embarrassment today. The adoption of the trapeze and the spinnaker for instance risks declassing ten thousand boats. Finding a successor to the Star in the line-up of Olympic classes will not however be an easy job. Even if such a boat is more easily trailed, faster down wind, cheaper, and in short more modern, it is most unlikely that it will be any finer an instrument to sail to windward. A windward thrash in a Star is a thrash indeed.

Star Class. LOA: 22 ft. 9 in. LWL: 15 ft. 6 in. Beam: 5 ft. 9 in. Draft: 3 ft. 4 in. Sail area: 281 sq. ft. Displacement: 1,459 lb.

The Strange Affair of the One Ton Cup and the 5·5-Metre Class

International 5·5-Metre Class
(Average dimensions)
LOA: *31 ft.*
LWL: *25 ft.*
Beam: *6 ft. 6 in.*
Draft: *4 ft. 5 in.*
Sail area: *300 sq. ft.*
Displacement: *3,840 lb.*

IN 1898 a cup was presented for racing in boats whose keels weighed one ton. In 1899 it was won by the French boat *Belouga*. The trophy was then transferred in 1908 to the 6-Metres (an earlier formula than the International Rule) and later to the 6·5-Metres. The International Rule governed the 6·5s, introducing a new principal in rule making. The mathematics read:

$$\frac{L + \tfrac{1}{4}G + 2d + \sqrt{S} - F}{2\cdot 5}$$

but the rule itself was, so to speak, less important than its restrictions, limits and annexed penalties. It worked out that everything had its price: the scantlings of the hull, the displacement which should not be less than a certain tonnage in proportion to the waterline length, the fullness of the sections in the run and so on. Hollows in the lines were barred, there was a minimum freeboard figure and a maximum one for draft. There was a control on the height of the sail plan and the shape of the mast and boom. The construction of the mast was the subject of detailed minima. It all sounds very complicated but in fact the rule produced a stable and flourishing situation across a span of thirty-five years.

Our photograph on page 175 was taken in the One Ton Cup series of 1921 which was won by the remarkable British boat *Cordella* (K1) from the Dutch *Oranje II*. However, Holland managed to win the Cup in 1924 and kept it up to 1926.

Thereafter the One Ton Cup was again transferred—this time to the 6-Metres (International Rule). In this class there were to be many famous trophy-winning boats—boats like the Swedish *Maybe VI*, the American *Llanoria*, the Swiss *Ylliam IX* and the French *Elghi III*. Now the One Ton Cup, thanks to an inspired idea of the Cercle de la Voile de Paris, has taken up a new career as the major trophy of the offshore yachts at the 22 feet R.O.R.C. rating level. A new chapter has been opened. This will demonstrate once again the influence of top class competition on the development of the design and construction of yachts—as well as an architect's ability to read a rule.

This decision has blocked the award of the One Ton Cup to the 5·5-Metre Class. These were born out of a feeling that the wonderful 6-Metres would have to give way in the end to a lighter and less costly boat. The great Charles E. Nicholson and Maldon Heckstall-Smith had in their minds a compromise between the heavy 6-Metres and the light 30 Square Metres Skerry Cruisers, and this rule, adopted by the International Yacht Racing Union, produced the out-and-out racing boats which one can admire on pages 182 and 183.

The 5·5-Metre has been an Olympic listed class since 1956. Indeed it is said that these boats with their short keels were specially designed for the Naples Olympics; another story goes that their modest draft of a shade under 4 ft. 6 in. was the result of Dutch insistence that deeper draught would be unacceptable in the Ijsell Meer—and no doubt both stories are incorrect.

As has happened before in the 'Metre Boat' field, research into the ramifications of the rule has thrown up certain designers who appear to have got the best out of the rule—quickest. The first to come to the fore were the Swedish boats from the drawing-boards of Laurin and Ohlsen. Since 1960 American designs have come up in the world. A Ray Hunt design *Minotaur* in the hands of George O'Day won the Gold Medal at the Naples Olympics of that year. Ohlsen, however, probably still gets as much of the business as any designer, and the 1968 British Olympic Bronze Medallist at Acapulco, Robin Aisher, built an Ohlsen boat.

In 1964 at the Tokyo Olympics the Australians

carried off the 5·5 Gold Medal with *Barranjoey* and their boat was designed by the American, Bill Luders. For the first time alloy masts and moulded wood hulls appeared.

In 1967 another American designer moved to the 'top of the pops' with 5·5-Metre owners. He was Britton Chance, and the boat that started the trend was his *Cloud B,* which carried off the World Championship of that year. Most boats from here on were to be of moulded wood. Some at this stage had advanced so far in sophistication as to have provision for the ejection below the waterline of polymers to reduce surface friction, but the International Yacht Racing Union put paid to that idea. It is this sort of sophistication than can destroy a class and confine it to a handful of 'win-at-all-costs-and-damn-the-expense' owners.

The British champion Robin Aisher's first 5·5, *Yeoman,* weighed 4,520 lb. of which 2,350 lb.

was in the ballast keel. *Yeoman XV* displaced exactly the same poundage in total but ways and means had been found to increase the ballast component of the all-up weight to 3,615 lb. The 5·5-Metres are the most tank-tested models of any class—and this factor alone could explain the advance of the Americans in the field of 5·5-Metre design. One can also understand that amateur designers in a class where the smallest alteration in the lines has to be carefully tested in the tank have a pretty thin time. However, you can't get away from the fact that Britton Chance, who started with amateur status, has just designed two 12-Metres!

The 5·5-Metre class is not included in the Olympic list for 1972. Is it the shrinking of private wealth or the bureaucratic spirit that wishes to bring everything down to a common level that condemns such an exciting class . . . ?

Swallow Class
LOA: *25 ft. 6 in.*
LWL: *19 ft.*
Beam: *5 ft. 7 in.*
Draft: *3 ft. 6in.*
Sail area: *200 sq. ft.*
Displacement: *Approx. 2,000 lb.*

To Dethrone the Star...

THE competition was declared open— and a fair number of naval architects sent in their ideas for a two-man keel boat. Uffa Fox designed *Pensive Temptress* (which was almost immediately dubbed 'Expensive Temptress') but although a first class design (later to bear fruit in the 'Flying series' of which the Flying Fifteen is the most successful) the choice fell on the gifted amateur Tom Thornycroft, who put forward the Swallow design.

The Swallow is a one-design as to hull form and weight, and weight of mast. Within 200 sq. ft. limitation on sail area, variations are permitted in spars, rigging and the configuration of the cockpit. The sail area maximum leads of course to a jib of moderate dimension in contrast to the extreme overlap of some genoas in other classes—and this is a *Good Thing!*

The Swallow is 25 ft. 6 in. overall, 19 ft. on the waterline and draws 3 ft. 6 in. This design was chosen as a two-man keel boat for the 1948 Olympics at Torquay, but the fourteen teams were not wildly enthusiastic about the boat and by the 1952 Games the class had been dropped. All the same she is a good, sporty boat, probably better suited to a three-man crew than the two-man she was originally planned for. But fashions in boats come and go like—well, like fashions. Classes are born and they die—and then again, the old Star is not that easily eclipsed.

The International Dragon Class

LOA: 29 ft. 2 in.
LWL: 18 ft. 7 in.
Beam: 6 ft. 5 in.
Draft: 3 ft. 9¾ in.
Sail area: 215 sq. ft.
Displacement: 4,480 lb.

A SEA full of white horses, a boisterous Force 6 brewing up and the Solent in fighting form. Most boats will have taken a reef in and their skippers will be thinking of getting back to a sheltered mooring. That's not so with this Dragon and her crew. Here's a day for planing under a taut spinnaker — and here's the type of boat that literally rejoices in choppy seas and fresh winds.

This Dragon is the successful *Penguin Too* owned by Bruce Donald. She was often sailed by a woman, Pepe Stratton (née Lowles), the daughter of a notable statesman of the yachting world Sir Geoffrey Lowles and wife of an equally notable Finn helmsman, Vernon Stratton. The latter was team manager for the successful British effort at the Mexico Olympics in 1968. His wife Pepe was his assistant.

The story of the Dragon Class is a story indeed. She was designed by the Norwegian naval architect Johan Anker in 1929, only one of a great number of one-designs produced in Scandinavia for weekend cruising and racing. In 1948 with the support of the Scandinavians, Germans, and British, the Dragon was adopted as an Olympic class in the three-man keel boat category. Immediately the racing men of the world seized on it and gave the design what might be termed 'the treatment'. The cabin top was reduced to the very minimum and the cabin itself with all its appointments was totally suppressed. Shrouds and stays passed through the deck in all sorts of spots in order to match up with gadgets and gear — and of course there was some pretty complicated rule making.

As an Olympic one-design the Dragon has confirmed her excellent reputation as being a hard-weather boat — one to stand up to her canvas and one that could be really pushed to windward in spite of a tendency to slam in a chop. Judged by modern criteria the Dragon is a slow boat — particularly in light airs. The rigging plan is dated and the spinnaker a small sail indeed, while her displacement and dimensions make her difficult to move around in an age when international encounters are the order of the day. But given a capful of wind and a sparkle of sun and a bit of a sea and a close-fought race in the Dragon class — that's something!

The End of the Metre Story

BY THE 1960s the various 'Metre rules and ratings', which in one form or another had dominated yacht racing for so long, had virtually declined to the 12-Metres and the 5·5-Metres—the former restricted for all practical purposes to challengers for the America's Cup and veterans from past challenges, the latter already dealt a bodyblow by the decision of the Olympic Committee.

But the One Designs, or rather the one-design line of thought, continues to prosper. Indeed, such classes have become so well established that newer and more vigorous arrivals on the scene have found it a tough job to dislodge the 'sitting tenants', however much improved might be the sport they have to offer. But either way, they had started to lose the eye of Keith Beken's camera. They lacked novelty and change, the drama of new rigs and new sail plans.

Instead, his interests turned to the ocean racers and the offshore scene the Fastnet, Newport–Bermuda, Sydney–Hobart boats. And the history of those races and the boats which took part in them is another Beke story to be told. . . .

Index